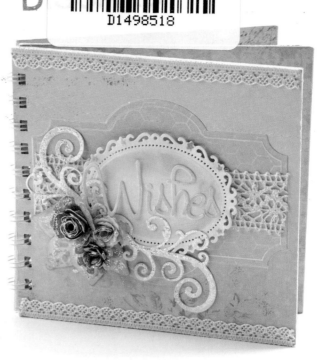

I always enjoy presenting those nearest and dearest to me with beautifully handcrafted gifts.

Creating personalized gifts that are crafted from the heart is the ultimate expression of love. It brings me such joy to see the expressions of surprise and delight my gifts bring to those receiving them!

I'd like to share the pleasure of creating one-of-a-kind gifts so you, too, can make beautiful creations for those you love. *Spellbinders™ Giftabilities* provides a stunning collection of gift-worthy projects designed to ensure a creative and successful crafting experience! Each chapter in this book contains a dazzling array of ideas perfect for every skill level. Come grow your creativity as we show you how one Spellbinders design element can be used to create beginner, intermediate and advanced professionally finished projects.

Spellbinders Giftabilities will teach you how to use our award-winning products and inspire you to create stunning, handcrafted gifts. I'm so excited that our Spellbinders Nestabilities® Majestic Elements, used to create the dazzling ornaments in this book, won the prestigious 2012 Summer Craft & Hobby Association Innovations Award! Included is a special chapter with tips, techniques and different mediums showing you the endless possibilities when using Spellbinders crafting tools. With easy-to-follow instructions, complete materials lists and step-by-step photography, you will learn how to create beautiful jewelry, ornaments, frames, memory albums, keepsake boxes and more! Discover all the innovative and fun Spellbinders designs you can use to personalize your handcrafted gifts.

I'd like to extend a very special thank you to our multitalented and gifted designers featured in this book. We truly have the best designers in the industry and they have outdone themselves in showing how our crafting tools can be used by all skill levels to create beautiful projects perfect for gifts! The value and versatility of our innovative craft tools allow for creativity without limitation. It is my pleasure to continue developing the very best cutting, embossing and stenciling tools.

Enjoy your crafting adventure,

Stacey Caron

Stacey Caron *is the creative force behind Spellbinders innovative designs and product lines. She has been scrapbooking and stamping for many years, and her enthusiasm for paper crafts truly inspires others. She has taught throughout the United States and internationally for retailers, private groups, scrapbook and stamping stores, distributors and sales groups. In 2012, Stacey was selected to receive an Enterprising Women Award. The Annual Enterprising Women of the Year Awards recognizes the finest women entrepreneurs in North America and beyond. It is widely considered one of the most prestigious recognition programs for female business owners. Stacey and her husband, Jeff, have been married for 18 years and live in sunny Arizona with their two sons, Nathan and Justin.*

CONTENTS

Spellbinders™ Giftabilities

EDITOR Tanya Fox

CREATIVE DIRECTOR Brad Snow

PUBLISHING SERVICES DIRECTOR
Brenda Gallmeyer

MANAGING EDITOR Brooke Smith

GRAPHIC DESIGNER Nick Pierce

COPY SUPERVISOR Deborah Morgan

COPY EDITORS Emily Carter,
Samantha Mawhorter

TECHNICAL EDITOR Corene Painter

PHOTOGRAPHY SUPERVISOR Tammy Christian

PHOTO STYLISTS Tammy Liechty,
Tammy Steiner

PHOTOGRAPHY Matthew Owen

PRODUCTION ARTIST SUPERVISOR
Erin Brandt

PRODCUTION ARTIST Nicole Gage

PRODUCTION ASSISTANTS Marj Morgan,
Judy Neuenschwander

Spellbinders Giftabilities is published by
Annie's, 306 East Parr Road, Berne, IN 46711.
Printed in USA. Copyright © 2012 Annie's. All
rights reserved. This publication may not be
reproduced in part or in whole without written
permission from the publisher.

RETAIL STORES: If you would like to carry this
pattern book or any other Annie's publication,
visit AnniesWSL.com.

Every effort has been made to ensure that the
instructions in this publication are complete
and accurate. We cannot, however, take
responsibility for human error, typographical
mistakes or variations in individual work. Please
visit AnniesCustomerCare.com to check for
pattern updates.

ISBN: 978-1-59635-571-2
Printed in the USA
1 2 3 4 5 6 7 8 9

4 Special Techniques

Capturing Memories

Creative Cards

Gift Sets

Happy Holidays

Home Decor

Jewelry

Mixed Media

Exquisite Ornaments

Die Cutting

Cut shapes with Spellbinders™ die templates by creating a die-cutting sandwich.

1. Stack items in the following order: Base Plate; die template, cutting edge up; cardstock; and Cutting Plate (photo 1).

2. Keeping the sandwich flat and straight, insert it into the Spellbinders™ Grand Calibur® die-cutting/embossing machine. Turn the handle until the sandwich exits the other side of the machine (photo 2).

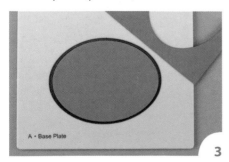

3. Remove the sandwich.

4. Open the sandwich to reveal the die-cut piece (photo 3).

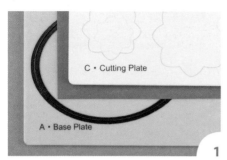

Tip: *Save the die-cut window piece for another project!*

Embossing

To emboss die-cut shapes, create an embossing sandwich with the die-cut shape still placed within the die template.

1. Stack items in the following order: Base Plate; die template, cutting edge up with cut cardstock still in die template; Embossing Mat; and Embossing Plate (photo 4).

2. Keeping the sandwich flat and straight, insert it into the die-cutting/embossing machine. Turn the handle until the sandwich exits the other side of the machine.

3. Remove the sandwich.

4. Open the sandwich to reveal the die-cut/embossed shape (photo 5).

Die Cutting & Embossing Stamped Images

Getting perfect placement to cut stamped images with Spellbinders™ die templates is so simple!

1. Stamp an image onto paper or cardstock.

2. Place die template over stamped image, cutting side down; center die for perfect placement (photo 6).

3. Use repositionable tape to secure die template onto paper or cardstock.

4. Run through die-cutting/embossing machine to cut. Follow Embossing instructions to emboss this piece if desired (photo 7).

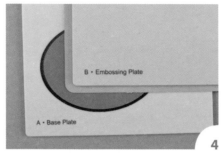

Tip: *Tape die template to paper on outer edge of die template to avoid damage to stamped image.*

Did You Know?

Nestabilities® dies are numbered to make identifying the correct size easy. #1 will always be the smallest die template in the set.

Embossing With M-Bossabilities™

Create embossed patterns by using M-Bossabilities™ embossing folders.

1. Stack items in the following order: Base Plate, embossing folder with paper inside and D Adapter Plate (photo 8).

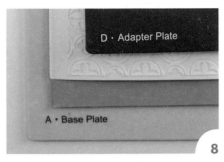

2. Keeping the sandwich flat and straight, insert it into the die-cutting/embossing machine. Turn the handle until the sandwich exits the other side of the machine.

3. Remove the sandwich.

4. Open the sandwich; open the embossing folder to reveal the embossed paper (photo 9).

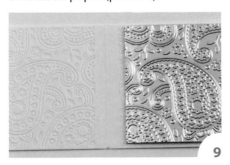

Extending Embossed Areas

It's easy to extend your embossed surface when using M-Bossabilities™ with a uniform pattern!

1. Cut desired size of paper. *Note: Limit the width of paper to the width of the die-cutting machine.*

2. Place paper in embossing folder; run through die-cutting/embossing machine (photo 10).

3. Open folder, move paper on M-Bossabilities™ embossing folder so that only one row of previously embossed area is in the cavity of the embossing folder. Close folder over un-embossed area (photo 11).

4. Run through machine again.

5. Repeat steps 3 and 4 until piece of paper is fully embossed.

Sanding Embossed Areas

When working with white core cardstock or foils, try sanding the embossed areas to create a unique look!

1. Emboss white core cardstock or craft foil using desired embossing folder (photo 12).

2. Gently sand embossed area using sandpaper or a sanding block with a circular motion to see the inner color pop (photo 13).

Making a Shaped Card

Why be limited to standard-shape cards when you can use Spellbinders™ die templates to make custom-shaped cards?

1. Fold cardstock in half to form a card base slightly larger than selected die template.

2. Place folded edge of cardstock inside die template cutting line (photo 14).

3. Use repositionable tape to secure die template to cardstock.

4. Run through die-cutting/embossing machine to create a custom-shaped and embossed card (photo 15).

Making Frames

Create the perfect paper frame without the tedious work of using a craft knife. Spellbinders™ Nestabilities® die templates make the process super simple!

1. Choose two die templates in desired shapes.

2. Secure larger die template to cardstock with repositionable tape. This will be the outside edge of the frame.

3. Nest smaller die template inside larger die template; secure with repositionable tape. This will make the opening of the frame (photo 16).

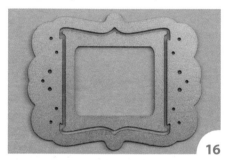

16

4. Run through die-cutting machine to create a custom-shaped frame (photo 17).

17

Using Die Templates as Stencils

To get a great finished look, try this fun technique!

1. Die-cut and emboss cardstock with die template.

2. Leave cardstock in die template with cutting side down.

3. Apply ink or chalk to cardstock through open areas of die template (photo 18).

18

4. Remove cardstock from die template (photo 19).

19

Reverse Stenciling

Add color to die templates to change the look of your die cuts by reverse stenciling! Create colored borders from Nestabilities® and colored fields within Shapeabilities® die templates.

1. Apply ink generously to cutting side of die template (photo 20).

20

2. Die-cut and emboss as usual.

3. The die cut will be inked in all areas covered by inked die template (photo 21).

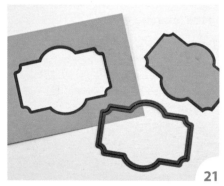

21

Did You Know?

Frames created with Spellbinders™ die templates make great frames for photos on scrapbook pages.

Selective Die Cutting

Stretch your creativity in die cutting! Try selective cutting to further customize your crafts.

1. Place cardstock, felt or other medium over die template. Secure in place with repositionable tape (photo 22).

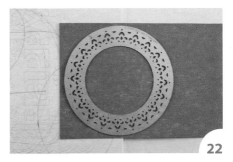

2. Run through die-cutting/ embossing machine with part of the die extending over the end of the mats to create a custom die-cut image (photo 23).

Making a Spiral Flower

Create pretty paper blossoms with die-cut flower shapes.

1. Cut and emboss Bitty Blossom from desired paper or cardstock.

2. Remove paper from die template (photo 24).

3. Roll flower petals starting on the outside of the die-cut piece (photo 25).

4. Adhere rolled flower base section of die-cut piece (photo 26).

Tip: Use a toothpick to begin rolling process on small flowers. Use a pencil to begin rolling process on larger spiral flowers.

Creating a Fancy Medallion

Take your crafting skills to a new level when you create this intricate medallion embellishment.

1. Cut and emboss 13 #2 Splendid Circles from clear vellum or desired medium.

2. Fold a cut/embossed circle in half (photo 27).

3. In the same manner as folding a paper airplane, fold the inside edges of circle down until the scalloped edge just touches the outside edge of folded circle (photo 28). ***Note:*** *This will create a folded diagonal edge (photo 29).*

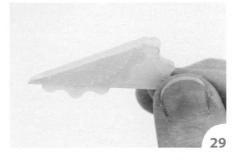

4. Press down on diagonal folds from step 3, pressing them toward center fold. When finished, the folded edges from step 3 should align over center fold from step 2 (photo 30).

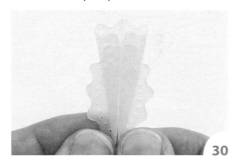

5. Cut a #2 Splendid Circle from vellum and one from an adhesive sheet. Adhere die-cut pieces together.

6. Adhere flat side of folded circles to adhesive side of die cut from step 5, making sure to adhere pointed edge of folded circle to center of adhesive circle (photo 31).

7. Continue adhering folded circles to die cut from step 5, aligning edges with piece adhered before it (photo 32).

8. Once all folded circles have been adhered, lift up top folded edge of each folded circle to create a dimensional look (photo 33).

Special Jewelry-Making Techniques

Spellbinders™ die templates are such versatile products that they can even be used to create one-of-a-kind jewelry components. Both pendant and earring projects are featured in this book. To create these projects you will need to know a few basic jewelry-making techniques.

Creating a Simple Loop

1. Holding head pin with round-nose pliers above the beads, bend wire 90 degrees just above the beads. Trim excess to ¼ inch (photo 34).

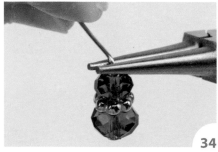

2. Grasp end of wire with round-nose pliers and roll into a loop. Remove and replace pliers into the loop as needed to finish the loop (photo 35).

3. Adjust loop as desired (photo 36).

Creating a Wrapped Loop Link

1. Grasp 4-inch length of wire 1 inch from end with round-nose pliers. Bend wire to 90-degree angle over top of pliers (photo 37).

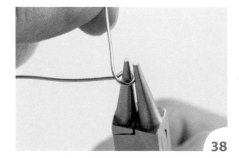

2. Place pliers above the bend. Pull wire around round-nose pliers until it crosses in front of itself, forming a loop; reposition pliers as needed (photo 38).

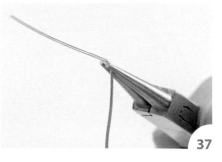

3. Place round-nose pliers into loop, wrap tail of wire around wire stem until entire tail has been wrapped; trim tail as close to wrap as possible. Press end of wire into wrap (photo 39).

4. On opposite end of wire, grasp wire above wrap with round-nose pliers. Bend wire to 90-degree angle over top of pliers. Repeat step 2 (photo 40).

5. Thread pendant or desired component onto wire and slide into loop (photo 41).

6. Wrap tail of wire around stem of wire and over previous wrap. Continue wrapping wire over wrap until desired messy wrap has been created. Trim wire as close to wrap as possible and press end of wire into wrap (photo 42).

How to Create a Wrapped Loop Dangle

1. Thread desired beads onto a head pin (photo 43).

2. Grasp wire above beads with round-nose pliers; bend wire 90 degrees just above the beads. Repeat steps 2 and 3 of Creating a Wrapped Loop Link instructions (photo 44).

3. Wrap tail of wire around wire stem until entire tail has been wrapped; trim tail as close to wrap as possible. Press end of wire into wrap (photo 45).

How to Open & Close a Jump Ring

1. Hold one half of jump ring with opening at the top (photo 46).

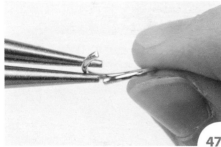

2. With round-nose pliers, grasp opposite side of jump ring and twist (photo 47).

3. To close, twist back (photo 48).

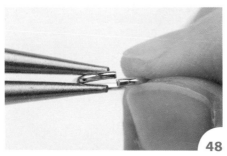

Capturing
Memories

Prom Magic

DESIGNS BY **LATISHA YOAST**

Decorative Canvas

Project notes: *Refer to photo for placement throughout. Use foam squares to adhere labels and photos to canvas. For added dimension, use a double layer of foam squares.*

Using #5 Grand Large Labels die template, cut and emboss a label from patterned paper. Using #3 Grand Large Labels die template, cut and emboss a label from a photo. Adhere labels together, placing foam squares on corners of photo only. Adhere layered labels to canvas.

Using #2 Grand Large Labels die template, cut and emboss a label from patterned paper. Using #1 Grand Large Labels die template, cut and emboss a label from a photo. Layer and adhere labels to canvas.

Adhere a 3 x 2-inch photo to canvas.

Using #1 Grand Large Labels die template, cut and emboss a label from white cardstock. Attach "prom" stickers to top edge of white label. Wrap twine horizontally around label three times. Tie a bow and trim ends. Secure bow in place with an adhesive dot. Adhere label to canvas, sliding it behind large photo label.

Thread buttons with twine as desired, tying bows in front or knots on back. Adhere buttons to canvas with adhesive dots.

Sources: *Die templates and die-cutting/ embossing machine from Spellbinders™ Paper Arts; burlap canvas from Canvas Corp.; cardstock from Bazzill Basics Paper Inc.; patterned paper from Carta Bella; Thickers alphabet stickers from American Crafts; baker's twine from The Twinery; foam squares and adhesive dots from SCRAPBOOK ADHESIVES BY 3L™.*

Materials
Spellbinders™
- Nestabilities® Grand Large Labels die templates (#LF-168)
- Grand Calibur®

Additional
- 12 x 12-inch burlap canvas
- White cardstock
- Paris Girl Le Grande Tour patterned paper
- Photos
- Black glitter alphabet sticker
- Pink buttons
- Hot pink baker's twine
- Adhesive foam squares
- Adhesive dots

Did You Know?
To create a hidden pocket for journaling, pop up a picture or patterned paper so the journaling spot fits perfectly.

Materials
Spellbinders™
- Nestabilities® Grand Large Labels die templates (#LF-168)
- Grand Calibur®

Additional
- Kraft cardstock
- Paris Girl Le Grande Tour patterned paper
- 2 x 3-inch photo
- Burlap
- Black glitter alphabet stickers
- Pink buttons
- 24 inches ⅝-inch-wide hot pink sheer satin-edge ribbon
- ³⁄₁₆-inch hole punch
- Adhesive foam squares
- Adhesive dots

Mini Book

Using #3 Grand Large Labels die template, cut two labels from burlap and two labels from cardstock. Adhere each burlap label to a cardstock label, creating front and back covers for mini book.

Using same die template, cut and emboss multiple labels from cardstock. **Note:** *These will be the pages for the mini book.*

Using #2 Grand Large Labels die template, cut and emboss a label from patterned paper. Attach to front cover with foam squares.

Lay front cover, pages and back cover on top of each other. Referring to photo for placement, punch two holes through one short edge of stacked pieces. **Note:** *If stacked pieces are too thick to punch through all layers, try stacking only a few pieces at a time. Then use punched pieces as a template to mark where to punch remaining pages.*

Cut ribbon into two 12-inch lengths. Thread a length of ribbon through each set of holes; tie bows and trim ends.

Adhere photo to burlap; trim a small border. Attach to front cover using a double layer of foam squares.

Attach "so fun" stickers to front cover. Embellish front cover with buttons as desired, using adhesive dots.

Add photos and favors to pages as desired. ■

Sources: *Die templates and die-cutting/embossing machine from Spellbinders™ Paper Arts; cardstock from Bazzill Basics Paper Inc.; patterned paper from Carta Bella; burlap from Canvas Corp.; Thickers alphabet stickers from American Crafts; foam squares and adhesive dots from SCRAPBOOK ADHESIVES BY 3L™.*

Capturing Memories Frame

Did You Know?
You can frame your photos using Grand Labels die templates.

DESIGN BY **JULIE OVERBY**

Project notes: *Distress and ink edges of cut pieces as desired. Refer to photo throughout for placement of elements.*

Adhere an 11½ x 11½-inch piece of cream patterned paper to a 12 x 12-inch piece of kraft cardstock, creating a page base.

Cut a 3½ x 11-inch piece from Stationery paper. Adhere to page base.

Using Motif LG Vintage Lace Motifs die template, cut a motif from cream patterned paper; leave die template in place. Referring to Using Die Templates as Stencils

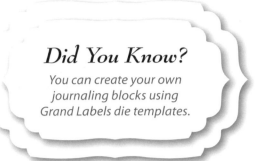

Did You Know?

You can create your own journaling blocks using Grand Labels die templates.

Materials

Spellbinders™
- Nestabilities® die templates: Grand Large Labels (#LF-168), Blossom Five (#S4-370)
- Shapeabilities® die templates: Lattice Motifs (#S5-107), Vintage Lace Motifs (#S5-109), Les Papillions (#S4-371), Ribbon Banners LG (#S5-122)
- Edgeabilities® Classic Edges One die templates (#E8-007)
- Grand Calibur®

Additional
- Cardstock: kraft, brown with colored core
- Patterned papers: Botanique Stationery, Botanique Grandma's Pearls, cream
- Photo
- Large frame
- Brown alphabet stickers
- Light brown distress ink pad
- Black fine-tip marker
- 8 inches ¾-inch-wide cream lace trim
- Cream twine
- White button
- Cream self-adhesive pearls
- Sanding block or sandpaper
- Blending tool
- Adhesive runner
- Adhesive dots
- Adhesive foam dots
- Double-sided adhesive

technique and using light brown ink, add ink to die cut. Repeat twice for a total of three inked motifs. ***Note:*** *If desired, die-cut one motif and cut into pieces and adhere to page base as desired.*

Using Scalloped Classic Edges One die template, cut one long edge of a 1½ x 8-inch piece of brown cardstock. Adhere to back left edge of an 8½ x 8½-inch piece of Stationery paper. Adhere to page base.

Using Motif Lattice Motifs die template, cut and emboss a motif from cream patterned paper; leave die template in place and ink in the same manner as before. Cut off edge from side of die cut and adhere to page base. Cut a 4-inch piece of lace trim and adhere to cut edge of motif.

Using desired Les Papillions butterfly die template, cut and emboss a butterfly from cream patterned paper; leave die template in place and ink in the same manner as before. Adhere to page base and embellish with pearls.

Using #2 Grand Large Labels die template, cut and emboss a label from brown cardstock. Cut and emboss a #1 Grand Large Labels from Grandma's Pearls paper. Write desired journaling text onto label with fine-tip marker. Referring to photo, create sentiment along top of sentiment label with alphabet stickers. Adhere lace trim along bottom of sentiment label. Adhere labels together and set aside.

Using #1 Grand Large Labels die template, cut and emboss a label from photo. Cut and emboss a #2 Grand Large Label from cream patterned paper. Cut and emboss a #3 Grand Large Label from brown cardstock; distress edges with sanding block. Adhere labels together.

Layer and adhere sentiment panel, photo panel and remaining motifs to page base.

Using #3 Ribbon Banners LG, cut and emboss a label from cream patterned paper. Cut off left edge of banner. Hand-write desired sentiment onto banner with fine-tip marker. Attach to page base with foam dots.

Using #3 Blossom Five die template, cut and emboss a flower from cream patterned paper; leave die template in place and ink in the same manner as before. Repeat to cut a second flower using #2 Blossom Five die template. Layer and adhere flowers to page base with adhesive dots.

Thread button with twine; tie bow on front, trim ends. Attach to flower using an adhesive dot.

Secure finished page inside frame. ■

Sources: *Die templates and die-cutting/embossing machine from Spellbinders™ Paper Arts; kraft cardstock from American Crafts; Tim Holtz Distress colored core cardstock from Core'dinations; Botanique patterned paper from G.C.D. Studios; Tiny Type alphabet stickers from Cosmo Cricket; Alpha Stickers from Webster's Pages; distress ink pad from Ranger Industries Inc.; self-adhesive pearls from Want2Scrap; adhesive runner from SCRAPBOOK ADHESIVES BY 3L™; adhesive dots from Glue Dots; double-sided adhesive from Scor-Pal Products.*

Art Journal

DESIGN BY **JUDY HAYES**

Book Covers

Treat two sheets of copper foil with liver of sulfur mixture following manufacturer's instructions. Set aside.

Front Cover

Using #5 Grand Large Label die template, cut and emboss three labels from chipboard. Run one label through sticker maker and then adhere to a second label. Set aside labels.

Cut a 6 x 7½-inch piece from adhesive-backed craft foam. Adhere a treated piece of copper foil to adhesive side of craft foam piece.

Referring to Extending Embossed Areas technique, emboss foil-covered craft foam piece with Mystic embossing folder. Referring to Making Frames technique and using #5 and #1 Grand Large Labels, cut and emboss a frame from copper side of foil-covered craft foam piece. Sand or buff to desired color.

Materials
Spellbinders™
- Nestabilities® die templates: Grand Large Labels (#LF-168), Labels Twenty-One (#S5-027)
- Shapeabilities® die templates: Jewel Alphabet (#LF-014), Girlie Grunge Labels (#S5-084), Persian Motifs (#S5-079), Botanical Swirls and Accents (#S5-146)
- M-Bossabilities™ Mystic embossing folder (#EL-006)
- Grand Calibur®

Additional
- Teal cardstock
- Patterned papers: Tea for Two Tea Tins, Kraft Reflections collection
- Lightweight chipboard
- Black adhesive-backed craft foam sheet
- Copper engraving board
- 36–38g copper craft foil
- Mona's Sketchbook stamp set
- Ink pads: black fine-detail, assorted brown
- Copic® markers: BG45, BG53, BG72, E19, V28, YR27
- Clear embossing powder
- Buttons
- Mini round copper brads
- 49 inches ½-inch-wide white seam binding
- Liver of sulfur
- Sandpaper
- Scoring board
- Embossing heat tool
- Paper piercer
- Adhesive dots and mini dots
- Double-sided adhesive: ⅛-inch-wide, ¼-inch-wide, ½-inch-wide
- Linen hinging tape*
- Adhesive runner with ½-inch adhesive
- 9-inch-wide sticker maker with permanent adhesive

If linen hinging tape is not available, thin ribbon or fabric strips with glue can also be used.

To create flap, use #1 Grand Large Labels die template to cut and emboss label from engraving board. Referring to Selective Die Cutting technique and using #5 Labels Twenty-One die template, cut and emboss a curved edge along one short edge of engraving board label. Finished die-cut piece should measure 2½ inches from top to curved bottom. Repeat twice, cutting piece once from craft foam and once from desired patterned paper; set aside. ***Note:*** *Keep remaining half of patterned paper label.*

Sand edges of engraving board flap piece; pierce holes through bottom corners and insert brads.

Place copper front cover frame facedown on work surface. Position engraving board flap piece inside frame. Cut a strip of linen hinging tape the width of the flap. Adhere hinging tape across seam of flap and frame to create a hinge.

Remove adhesive backing from craft foam flap piece; adhere to back of engraving board flap. Adhere patterned paper flap to back of foam flap.

Apply permanent adhesive to both sides of single chipboard label. Remove backing from one side only and attach to backside of frame, being careful to not adhere the flap.

Using #1 Grand Large Labels die template, cut a label from blue patterned paper. Stamp sentiment at center top of label with black ink. Sprinkle with embossing powder; heat-emboss. Ink edges light brown. Adhere inside frame on front cover. Adhere remaining half of blue patterned paper label from earlier to front cover inside frame as shown.

Using "CREATE" Girlie Grunge Labels die template, cut and emboss a sentiment rectangle from engraving board. Sand as desired and adhere to cover inside frame as shown.

Using Motif 4 Points Persian Motif die template, cut and emboss a motif from engraving board; sand as desired. Using Accent Botanical Swirls and Accents die template, cut and emboss an accent piece from engraving board; sand as desired. Layer and adhere motif and accent to flap front as shown. Embellish with buttons.

Using "ART" Jewel Alphabet die templates, cut and emboss letters from engraving board; sand as desired. Adhere to front cover as shown.

Back Cover

Create a Back Cover frame in the same manner as Front Cover frame.

Using #2 Grand Large Labels die template, cut a label from blue patterned paper. Stamp script onto label using brown ink. Ink edges light brown. Adhere to backside of cover frame with script side showing through front of frame.

Apply adhesive to both sides of single chipboard piece. Remove backing from one side only and attach to backside of Back Cover.

Using desired Girlie Grunge Labels die templates, cut and emboss words from engraving board; sand as desired. Adhere to Back Cover inside frame as shown.

Set cover aside.

Book Pages

Cut a 7¼ x 11½-inch piece from kraft patterned paper. With long edge horizontal on scoring board, make two vertical score lines ⅛ inch apart at center of piece. Fold on each score line, aligning short edges of piece.

Referring to Making a Shaped Card technique and using #5 Grand Large Labels die template, cut a shaped card from folded piece. **Note:** *Place die template so long edge extends about ¼ inch beyond folded edge of paper.* Remove paper from die template and use scissors to finish cuts at fold edge.

Repeat process six times, creating a total of seven page units.

Apply ½-inch-wide double-sided adhesive along each fold on kraft side of pages; do not remove liner. Decorate pages as desired on non-kraft side.

Working on back side of a page unit, apply permanent adhesive to one half of each page unit. To do this, fold page in half with patterned sides facing. Keep cut edges even and apply adhesive. Do not get adhesive between score lines.

Remove backing from double-sided adhesive on two page units. Align edges and adhere page units together. Repeat until all page units are fastened together.

Apply adhesive to one side of double-layered chipboard piece set aside in Front Cover assembly. Adhere to kraft side of paper on what will be first page of book.

Repeat to attach double-layered chipboard piece from Back Cover assembly to kraft side of what will be last page of book.

Optional Book Pages Materials
Spellbinders™

- Shapeabilities® die templates: Creative Book Pages (#LF-001), Creative Book Pages Two (#LF-002), Venetian Motifs (#S5-119), Jewel Keys (#S5-099)
- M-Bossabilities™ So Trendy embossing folder (#ES-006)
- Grand Calibur®

Additional

- Cardstock: teal, rust
- Black shrinkable plastic
- Stamps: Letter Background, Lace Edge, Just Thoughts set, Urban Tapestry set, Nature's Discovery set, Mixed Media set, Stuff to Say set, Art is letting your fingers capture
- Ink pads: brown archival, black fine-detail, light brown distress, brown distress, black distress, blue distress
- Copic® markers: BG45, BG53, BG72, E19, V28, YR27
- Mini round copper brads
- Craft wire: copper 20-gauge, copper 28-gauge, bronze 20-gauge
- Adhesive foam tape

Sources: *Die templates, embossing folder and die-cutting/embossing machine from Spellbinders™ Paper Arts; cardstock from Bazzill Basics Paper Inc.; shrinkable plastic from Shrinky Dinks®; Letter Background and Lace Edge stamps from Penny Black Inc.; stamp sets, distress ink pads and embossing powder from Ranger Industries Inc.; remaining stamp from Quietfire Designs; ColorBox archival ink pad from Clearsnap Inc.; VersaFine fine-detail ink pad from Imagine Crafts/Tsukineko; markers from Copic®/Imagination International Inc.; brads from Creative Impressions Inc.; craft wire from Artistic Wire; bamboo cord from Hemptique; adhesive foam tape from 3M.*

Ribbon Binding & Ties

Color seam binding with desired markers and inks. Dry with heat tool.

Apply ½-inch-wide double-sided adhesive across top and bottom of spine on page units extending ends onto first and last pages. Cut two short pieces of ribbon. Apply on top of double-sided adhesive. Apply another strip of ½-inch-wide double-sided adhesive across center of spine extending across width of first and last pages. Press ribbon onto adhesive, letting approximately 12 inches extend beyond pages for book closure ties.

Final Assembly

Remove backing from adhesive on back of Front Cover. Fasten to chipboard on front of page unit. Repeat for Back Cover. ■

Sources: *Die templates, embossing folder and die-cutting/embossing machine from Spellbinders™ Paper Arts; Tea for Two patterned paper from Cosmo Cricket; Kraft Reflections patterned paper from Graphic 45; copper engraving board from Royal & Langnickel; stamp sets, distress ink pads and embossing powder from Ranger Industries Inc.; VersaFine fine-detail ink pad from Imagine Crafts/Tsukineko; marker from Copic®/Imagination International Inc.; brads from Creative Impressions Inc.; Scor-Pal scoring board and double-sided adhesive from Scor-Pal Products; adhesive dots from Glue Dots; linen hinging tape from Lineco Inc.; Mega Runner adhesive runner and 9-inch Creative Station sticker maker from Xyron Inc.*

Creative Cards

For You

DESIGN BY **MICHELLE WOERNER**

Form a 5½ x 4¼-inch card from white cardstock.

Cut a 5½ x 1⅝-inch piece from turquoise patterned paper, a 5½ x 1¾-inch piece from white cardstock and a 5½ x 1⅞-inch piece from brown cardstock. Layer and adhere pieces to card front as shown.

Using #4 Splendid Circles die template, cut and emboss a circle from light brown cardstock; leave die template in place. Referring to Using Die Templates as Stencils technique, ink die cut light brown as shown.

In the same manner, cut and emboss a #2 circle from white cardstock; leave die template in place. Ink die cut light brown.

Cut and emboss a #3 circle from turquoise cardstock; leave die template in place. Using fine-tip black pen, color as shown.

Layer and adhere die-cut circles to card front as shown using foam tape. Adhere plastic flower to center of layered circles.

Stamp sentiment in black ink onto lower right corner of card.

Tie a bow with ribbon; trim ends. Adhere to card front as shown. ■

Sources: *Die templates and die-cutting/embossing machine from Spellbinders™ Paper Arts; cardstock and stamp set from Gina K. Designs; patterned papers from My Mind's Eye; ink pads from Clearsnap Inc.; ribbon from May Arts; plastic flower from Prima Marketing Inc.; foam tape from Elmer's® Products Inc.; liquid paper adhesive from Tombow USA.*

Materials
Spellbinders™
- Nestabilities® Splendid Circles die templates (#S4-354)
- Grand Calibur®

Additional
- Cardstock: white, brown, light brown, turquoise
- Follow Your Heart "Be Amazing" 6 x 6-inch paper pad
- Nature's Greetings stamp set
- Pigment ink pads: black, light brown
- Black fine-tip pen
- 13 inches 1-inch-wide turquoise satin-edge grosgrain ribbon
- Cabochon Collection peach plastic flower (#920975)
- Blending tool
- Adhesive foam tape
- Liquid paper adhesive

Hugs

DESIGN BY **DEBBIE OLSON**

Form a 5¼ x 5¼-inch card from white cardstock.

Cut a 5⅛ x 5⅛-inch piece from teal cardstock and a 4⅞ x 4⅞-inch piece from Newsprint paper. Sand edges of Newsprint panel and adhere to teal panel. Machine-stitch around edge of Newsprint panel. Adhere to card front.

Using #6 Lace Doily Motifs die template, cut and emboss a doily square from Un Billet paper. Adhere to card front as shown, only applying adhesive to center of die-cut piece; allow edge to hang free.

Using #4 Splendid Circles die template, cut and emboss a circle from white cardstock; leave die template in place. Referring to Using Die Templates as Stencils technique and using airbrush system, ink circle with BG93 and BG72 markers.

Thread ribbon through holes in circle. Tie a double bow and trim ends as shown. Attach to card front with foam tape.

Using #3 Splendid Circles die template, cut and emboss a circle from white smooth cardstock; leave die template in place. In the same manner as before, ink die cut lightly using airbrush system and BG72 marker. Before removing die template, stamp daisy image onto circle; remove die template. Stamp a second daisy image onto scrap piece of white smooth cardstock.

Color entire image on die-cut circle with markers; add detail with glitter pens as desired. **Note:** *The airbrushed pale blue-green in leaves will not hurt image; before coloring blossoms, however, you may want to use the Colorless Blender to push the blue-green out of the blossoms.* Only color one daisy on scrap piece of cardstock; cut out and adhere to die-cut image as shown with foam tape. Attach to card front with foam tape.

Using #1 Splendid Circles die template, cut and emboss a circle from white cardstock; leave die template in place. Ink using airbrush system and BG93 and BG72 markers. Remove die template and stamp sentiment onto circle.

Insert thread through top hole of sentiment circle. Thread under double bow and knot ends; trim if needed. Secure circle in place using foam tape. ■

Sources: Die templates and die-cutting/embossing machine from Spellbinders™ Paper Arts; white smooth cardstock, foam tape and double-sided tape from X-Press It; remaining cardstock from Papertrey Ink; patterned papers from Melissa Frances; stamp set from JustRite; Memento dye ink pad from Imagine Crafts/Tsukineko; markers, Colorless Blender, glitter pens and airbrush system from Copic®/Imagination International Inc.; ribbon from May Arts; adhesive dots from Therm O Web Inc.

Materials
Spellbinders™
- Nestabilities® Splendid Circles die templates (#S4-354)
- Shapeabilities® Lace Doily Motifs die templates (#S5-063)
- Grand Calibur®

Additional
- Cardstock: white smooth, white, teal
- C'est La Vie patterned papers: Newsprint, Un Billet
- Botanical Medallions and Banners stamp set
- Black dye ink pad
- Copic® markers: BG72, BG93, BV02, RV52, RV55, RV63, RV66, YG61, YG63, YR24, YR30, YR31
- Colorless Blender (0)
- Glitter pens: mint, buttermilk, clear
- 23 inches ¼-inch-wide white silk ribbon
- White cotton crochet thread
- Copic® airbrush system
- Sewing machine with white thread
- Sanding block or sand paper
- Adhesive foam tape
- Adhesive dots
- Double-sided tape

Elegant Medallion

DESIGN BY **BECCA FEEKEN**

Pocket

Cut a 4½ x 12-inch piece from patterned vellum. With long edge horizontal on scoring board, score a vertical line 6 inches from one short edge. Fold piece in half along scored line.

Referring to Selective Die Cutting technique and using #4 Splendid Circles die template, cut and emboss a half circle at top edge of folded vellum.

Unfold piece and score a line ¼ inch from each long edge; do not score along edge of die-cut section. Fold in at scored lines, creating a narrow flap along each long edge. Apply ⅛-inch-wide double-sided adhesive along flaps and re-fold piece, creating a pocket. **Note:** *Make sure opening of pocket is at least 4 inches wide.*

Wrap ribbon around pocket as shown; tie bow and V-notch ends. Adhere bow in place using a mini adhesive dot.

Thread one gold and one white pearl onto each corsage pin. Place earring backs onto ends of pins. Layer and adhere paper flower and pins to center of bow using hot glue. Let dry.

Fold down front die-cut section on top of pocket and tuck it behind bow, creating a decorative flap.

Materials
Spellbinders™
- Nestabilities® Splendid Circles die templates (#S4-354)
- Grand Calibur®

Additional
- Vellum: patterned, clear
- Kraft cardstock
- Patterned paper stacks: The Garden Tea Party, The Timeless Type
- Botanical Medallions and Banners stamp set
- Ink pads: brown distress, black pigment
- Clear fine-detail embossing powder
- 3 paper flowers
- 24 inches 1¼-inch-wide peach silk ribbon
- 2 white pearl corsage pins
- Glass pearls: 2 medium gold rondelle, 2 small white round
- 2 clear earring backs
- Self-adhesive flourishes: rhinestone, metal flourish
- Large white/gold pearl brad
- Small ivory self-adhesive pearls
- Antique gold round filigree
- Scoring board
- Blending tool
- Hot-glue gun
- Embossing heat tool
- Adhesive foam tape
- Mini adhesive dots
- 6 x 6-inch double-sided adhesive sheet
- ⅛-inch-wide double-sided adhesive

Card

Form a 3¾ x 4⅛-inch card from pink dot paper. Adhere a 3¾ x 4⅛-inch piece of pink dot paper inside card. Cut off top corners of card at an angle.

Cut two 3⅛ x 3½-inch pieces from text paper; ink edges brown. Adhere each text piece to kraft cardstock; trim a small border.

Referring to photo and using black ink, stamp desired sentiment for card front onto lower left corner of one text panel. In the same manner, stamp desired inside sentiment onto lower right corner of remaining panel. Sprinkle both sentiments with embossing powder; heat-emboss.

Embellish both sentiment panels with flourishes as shown. Adhere front sentiment panel to card front using foam tape. Adhere remaining sentiment panel inside card.

Using #4 Splendid Circles die template, cut and emboss a circle from light pink patterned paper; leave die template in place. Referring to Using Die Templates as Stencils, ink die cut brown. Remove die template and ink edges brown. Attach circle to card base as shown. Place small ivory pearls evenly around edge of circle.

Referring to Creating a Fancy Medallion technique, create a medallion, inking edges brown as desired.

Adhere finished medallion to large circle on card base by placing an adhesive dot on back outer edge of each folded circle.

Connect pearl brad to center of round filigree. Attach to center of fancy medallion using three layers of foam tape.

Insert card into pocket, allowing embellished circle to rest on outside of flap. ■

Sources: Die templates and die-cutting/embossing machine from Spellbinders™ Paper Arts; vellum and cardstock from Hobby Lobby Stores Inc.; patterned paper stacks from Die Cuts With A View; stamp set from JustRite; distress ink pad from Ranger Industries Inc.; VersaFine pigment ink pad from Imagine Crafts/Tsukineko; ribbon from May Arts; Recollections paper flowers, Recollections Signature Rhinestone stickers and filigree from Michaels Stores Inc.; Scor-Pal scoring board, double-sided adhesive sheet and double-sided adhesive from Scor-Pal Products; foam tape from 3M; adhesive dots from Glue Dots.

Gift Sets

Polka Dots Party Set

DESIGNS BY **AJ OTTO**

Materials
Spellbinders™
- Nestabilities® Labels Twenty-One die templates (#S5-027)
- Grand Calibur®

Additional
- Cardstock: white, turquoise, red
- Little Boy Awesome Dots patterned paper
- Ticket Trio stamp set
- Ink pads: blue pigment, black dye
- Red self-adhesive gems
- 4 inches ⅝-inch-wide white velvet ribbon
- Blending tool
- Adhesive foam squares
- Adhesive runner

Birthday Card

Form a 4¼ x 5½-inch card from turquoise cardstock. Adhere a 4 x 5¼-inch piece of patterned paper to card front.

Using #4 Labels Twenty-One die template, cut and emboss a label from turquoise cardstock. Cut and emboss a #3 label from red cardstock.

Stamp birthday sentiment onto white cardstock with black ink. Referring to Die Cutting & Embossing Stamped Images technique, cut and emboss a #2 label around sentiment; leave die template in place. Referring to Using Die Templates as Stencils technique and using blending tool, ink label blue.

Cut ends of ribbon into V-notches. Referring to photo and using foam squares as desired, layer and adhere die-cut labels and ribbon to card front.

Embellish sentiment label with gems.

Sources: Die templates and die-cutting/embossing machine from Spellbinders™ Paper Arts; cardstock from Stampin' Up! and American Crafts; patterned paper from Echo Park Paper Co.; stamp set from Gina K. Designs; ink pads and Stylus blending tool from Clearsnap Inc.; gems from Want2Scrap; ribbon from May Arts; paper crimper from Fiskars; foam squares and adhesive runner from SCRAPBOOK ADHESIVES BY 3L™.

Gift Tag

Form a 3¼ x 3¼-inch card from turquoise cardstock. Adhere a 3 x 3-inch piece of patterned paper to card front.

Using #3 Labels Twenty-One die template, cut and emboss two labels, one from turquoise cardstock and one from red cardstock. Layer and adhere labels to card front as shown, using foam squares as desired.

Cut and emboss a #2 label from white cardstock; leave die template in place. Referring to Using Die Templates as Stencils technique, ink label blue. Attach alphabet stickers to label to spell out name; embellish with gems. Attach to card front using foam squares.

Punch a hole through upper left corner of card. Thread ribbon through hole and tie a knot.

Sources: Die templates and die-cutting/embossing machine from Spellbinders™ Paper Arts; cardstock from Stampin' Up! and American Crafts; patterned paper from Echo Park Paper Co.; Tiny Type alphabet stickers from Cosmo Cricket; ink pad and Stylus blending tool from Clearsnap Inc.; gems from Want2Scrap; ribbon from May Arts; foam squares and adhesive runner from SCRAPBOOK ADHESIVES BY 3L™.

Materials
Spellbinders™
- Nestabilities® Labels Twenty-One die templates (#S5-027)
- Grand Calibur®

Additional
- Cardstock: white, turquoise, red
- Little Boy Awesome Dots patterned paper
- Alphabet stickers
- Blue pigment ink pad
- Red self-adhesive gems
- 8 inches ¼-inch-wide red satin ribbon
- Blending tool
- ⅛-inch hole punch
- Adhesive foam squares
- Adhesive runner

Treat Containers

Cut a 9 x 5½-inch piece from turquoise cardstock.

Apply adhesive to one short edge of cardstock piece. Adhere to opposite short edge, creating a tube.

Apply adhesive to one open end of cardstock tube, press edges together, closing one end of tube. Crimp closed end with paper crimper.

Fill tube with treats or gift.

Apply adhesive to open ends of tube. Press end closed in opposite direction of other end. Crimp edge using paper crimper.

Using #3 Labels Twenty-One die template, cut and emboss a label from patterned paper. Adhere to front of treat container.

Cut and emboss a #2 label from white cardstock; leave die template in place. Referring to Using Die Templates as Stencils technique, ink label blue. Attach alphabet stickers to label to spell treats. Attach to treat container using foam squares.

Materials
Spellbinders™

- Nestabilities® Labels Twenty-One die templates (#S5-027)
- Grand Calibur®

Additional

- Cardstock: white, turquoise
- Little Boy Awesome Dots patterned paper
- Alphabet stickers
- Blue pigment ink pad
- Blending tool
- Paper crimper
- Adhesive foam squares
- Adhesive runner

Sources: Die templates and die-cutting/embossing machine from Spellbinders™ Paper Arts; cardstock from Stampin' Up! and American Crafts; patterned paper from Echo Park Paper Co.; Tiny Type alphabet stickers from Cosmo Cricket; ink pad and Stylus blending tool from Clearsnap Inc.; paper crimper from Fiskars; foam squares and adhesive runner from SCRAPBOOK ADHESIVES BY 3L™.

Materials
Spellbinders™

- Nestabilities® Labels Twenty-One die templates (#S5-027)
- Grand Calibur®

Additional

- Cardstock: white, turquoise, red
- Little Boy Awesome Dots patterned paper
- Alphabet stickers
- Ticket Trio stamp set
- Ink pads: blue pigment, black dye
- Red self-adhesive gems
- Blending tool
- Adhesive foam squares
- Adhesive runner

Blanket Band

Cut two 2¼ x 12-inch pieces from white cardstock and two 1 x 12-inch pieces from red cardstock. Center and adhere red strips to white strips. Adhere short end of one layered strip to end of other layered strip, creating one long cardstock strip.

Using #4 Labels Twenty-One die template, cut and emboss a label from turquoise cardstock. Using #3 label die template, cut and emboss a label from patterned paper. Adhere labels together.

Stamp sentiment onto white cardstock with black ink. Referring to Die Cutting & Embossing Stamped Images and using #2 label die template, cut and emboss a label around sentiment; leave die template in place. Referring to Using Die Templates as Stencils technique, ink label blue. Adhere to layered labels and embellish with gems.

Adhere remaining short ends of layered cardstock strip to back of layered labels, creating a ring. ■

Sources: Die templates and die-cutting/embossing machine from Spellbinders™ Paper Arts; cardstock from Stampin' Up! and American Crafts; patterned paper from Echo Park Paper Co.; stamp set from Gina K. Designs; ink pads and Stylus blending tool from Clearsnap Inc.; gems from Want2Scrap; foam squares and adhesive runner from SCRAPBOOK ADHESIVES BY 3L™.

Wishes for Baby Gift Set

DESIGNS BY TINA MCDONALD

Materials
Spellbinders™
- Nestabilities® die templates: Labels Twenty-One (#S5-027), Floral Ovals (#S4-356)
- Grand Calibur®

Additional
- White cardstock
- Patterned papers: Attic Treasures Ledger Dot, C'est La Vie (Nana's Fabric, Aqua Doily, Hydrangeas)
- Chipboard alphabet
- Pigment ink pads: dark gray, yellow, blue, pink
- 20 inches ½-inch-wide white lace
- 33 inches ½-inch-wide white sheer ribbon
- Mini safety pins
- White eyelets
- ¹⁄₁₆-inch hole punch
- Eyelet-setting tool
- Blending tool
- 1½-inch create-a-sticker machine
- Adhesive foam squares

Baby Banner

Using #5 Labels Twenty-One die template, cut and emboss a label from each patterned paper for a total of four labels.

Cut four 5¼-inch lengths from lace. Run lace through create-a-sticker machine. Adhere a length of lace across center of each label.

Punch a ¹⁄₁₆-inch hole through each short edge of each label; attach eyelets.

Using #3 Floral Ovals die template, cut and emboss an oval from white cardstock; leave die template in place. Referring to Using Die Templates as Stencils, ink oval yellow. Repeat three more times, inking one oval pink, one blue and one gray. Adhere a chipboard letter to each oval spelling out "BABY." Using foam squares, adhere an oval to each label.

Cut sheer ribbon as follows: two (4½-inch) lengths and three (8-inch) lengths. Lay labels out on work surface in correct order. Connect labels together with longer lengths of ribbon by threading ribbon through eyelets and tying a bow; trim ends. Thread a 4½-inch length of ribbon through eyelet at end of banner. Tie ends of ribbon together creating a loop; trim ends. Repeat with opposite end of banner.

Attach mini safety pins to ribbon bows.

Sources: Die templates and die-cutting/embossing machine from Spellbinders™ Paper Arts; cardstock from WorldWin Papers; patterned papers from Melissa Frances; chipboard alphabet from Pink Paislee; ink pads from Clearsnap Inc.; sheer ribbon from Creative Impressions Inc.; create-a-sticker machine from Xyron; foam squares from SCRAPBOOK ADHESIVES BY 3L™.

Did You Know?

To make the banner sturdier, use the same die template to cut labels from empty cereal boxes. Adhere these labels to the backs of the paper labels before adding eyelets.

Materials
Spellbinders™
- Nestabilities® die templates: Labels Twenty-One (#S5-027), Floral Ovals (#S4-356)
- Shapeabilities® die templates: Bitty Blossoms (#S5-086), Jewel Flowers and Flourishes (#S5-143)
- Grand Calibur®

Additional
- White cardstock
- Assorted patterned papers: 5th Avenue Collection, C'est La Vie Collection
- 3 (6 x 6-inch) chipboard sheets
- Cappella Sticker Alphabets
- Ink pads: light purple pigment, blue pigment, brown distress, dark green distress
- White gel pen
- Iridescent glitter glue
- White lace: 12 inches ¼-inch-wide, 5¼ inches ½-inch-wide
- Book binding machine with ½-inch white coils
- Sanding block
- Blending tool
- 5-inch sticker maker with permanent adhesive
- 1½-inch create-a sticker machine
- Hot-glue gun
- Adhesive runner
- Adhesive foam squares

Baby Wishes Book

Cover front and back of chipboard squares with patterned paper. Trim edges evenly; sand edges. ***Note:*** *If desired, use lined patterned papers for inside pages.*

Following manufacturer's instructions, use book binding machine to bind book. ***Note:*** *Complete this process before decorating cover to prevent destroying embellishments.*

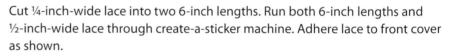

Using #5 Labels Twenty-One die template, cut and emboss a label from light aqua patterned paper; leave die template in place. Using gel pen, trace around inside edge of template onto label; remove template. Ink edges of label with gel pen. Run label through create-a-sticker machine; adhere to front cover as shown.

Cut ¼-inch-wide lace into two 6-inch lengths. Run both 6-inch lengths and ½-inch-wide lace through create-a-sticker machine. Adhere lace to front cover as shown.

Using #3 Floral Ovals die template, cut and emboss an oval from white cardstock; leave die template in place. Referring to Using Die Templates as Stencils, ink oval blue and light purple. Lightly ink "Wishes" alphabet stickers brown. Adhere to oval as shown. Attach to front cover using foam squares.

Using Flourish LG Jewel Flowers and Flourishes die template, cut and emboss two large flourishes from white cardstock. Apply glitter glue to flourishes; let dry. Run through create-a-sticker machine; adhere to front cover as shown.

Using desired sizes of Bitty Blossoms die templates, cut three flowers from pink and blue patterned papers. Referring to Making a Spiral Flower technique, roll and assemble flowers with hot glue.

Using Double Leaves Bitty Blossom die template, cut double leaf from light green patterned paper; leave die template in place. Ink leaves brown in the same manner as before; remove die template. Apply glitter glue as desired; let dry. Repeat once.

Layer and adhere flowers and leaves to front cover, using hot glue to attach flowers.

Sources: *Die templates and die-cutting/embossing machine from Spellbinders™ Paper Arts; cardstock from WorldWin Papers; patterned papers from Melissa Frances; alphabet stickers from BasicGrey; distress ink pads and glitter glue from Ranger Industries Inc.; gel pen from Sakura of America; sticker machines from Xyron; book binding machine from Zutter Innovative Products; adhesive runner and foam squares from SCRAPBOOK ADHESIVES BY 3L™.*

Welcome Baby Card

Form a 6 x 5-inch card from white cardstock. Referring to Making a Shaped Card technique and using #5 Labels Twenty-One die template, cut a shaped card from card base.

Referring to Making Frames technique and using #5 and #3 Labels Twenty-One die templates, cut and emboss a frame from Aqua Doily paper. Place a piece of Little Girls Collage paper onto back of frame, centering little girl image inside frame. Trim as needed and adhere in place. Adhere to card front, using 5-inch sticker maker.

Using Flourish LG and Flourish SM Jewel Flowers and Flourishes die templates, cut and emboss flourishes from white cardstock. Trim flourishes as desired, apply glitter glue; let dry. Adhere to card front as shown using 5-inch sticker maker.

Hand-print, or use computer to generate, "Welcome Baby" onto white cardstock. Using #2 ribbon Nested Lacey Pennants die template, cut and emboss a ribbon around sentiment; leave die templates in place. Referring to Using Die Templates as Stencils technique, ink sentiment ribbon light purple and dark green. Attach to card front as shown using foam squares.

Using Flower Med and Single Leaf SM Bitty Blossoms die templates, cut and emboss a flower and leaf from Jewell paper. Referring to Making a Spiral Flower technique, roll and assemble flowers using hot glue. Apply glitter glue to flower and leaf; let dry. Adhere to card front using hot glue. ∎

Sources: Die templates and die-cutting/embossing machine from Spellbinders™ Paper Arts; cardstock from WorldWin Papers; patterned papers from Melissa Frances; distress ink pads and glitter glue from Ranger Industries Inc.; sticker machines from Xyron; adhesive runner and foam squares from SCRAPBOOK ADHESIVES BY 3L™.

Materials
Spellbinders™
- Nestabilities® Labels Twenty-One die templates (#S5-027)
- Shapeabilities® die templates: Bitty Blossoms (#S5-086), Jewel Flowers and Flourishes (#S5-143), Nested Lacey Pennants (#S5-029)
- Grand Calibur®

Additional
- White cardstock
- Patterned papers: C'est La Vie (Aqua Doily, Little Girls Collage), 5th Avenue Jewell
- Ink pads: light purple pigment, brown distress, dark green distress
- Black fine-tip marker (optional)
- Blending tool
- Multicolored glitter glue
- Hot-glue gun
- 5-inch sticker maker
- Repositionable tape
- Adhesive runner
- Adhesive foam squares
- Computer with printer

Masquerade Gift Set

DESIGNS BY **KAZAN CLARK**

Mask

Project note: *Refer to photo throughout for placement.*

Using #4 Grand Labels Four, cut a label from black cardstock. Cut a #3 label from patterned paper. Adhere labels together, creating a mask base.

Referring to Reverse Stenciling technique, apply ink directly to outside edges of #3 Labels Twenty-One die template. Carefully position white cardstock over template; cut and emboss label. Repeat once.

Using #2 Tear Drop Circles die template, cut two teardrop circles from black cardstock. Center and adhere a tear drop circle to each white cardstock label. Adhere labels to mask base, only applying adhesive to center of labels.

Materials
Spellbinders™
- Nestabilities® die templates: Labels Twenty-One (#S5-027), Standard Circles LG (#S4-114), Grand Labels Four (#LF-190), Tear Drop Circles (#S4-344)
- Grand Calibur®

Additional
- Cardstock: black, white
- Enchanted Harlequin patterned paper
- Black fabric
- Black ink pad
- Self-adhesive rhinestones: medium clear, small amber
- Feathers: long red, decorative black with beads
- Red grosgrain ribbon in desired width
- 8½-inch-long wooden dowel
- Blending tool
- Hot-glue gun
- Repositionable tape
- Double-sided adhesive

Using #1 Standard Circles LG die template and using repositionable tape, secure die template in place over center of one black teardrop circle on mask base and cut. Repeat over remaining black teardrop circle.

Using #5 Standard Circles LG die template, cut a circle from black fabric. Use hot glue to adhere black feathers on back of circle along one half edge. While glue is still hot, fold fabric circle in half, pressing unfeathered edge into hot glue. Adhere to mask base as shown using hot glue.

Apply double-sided adhesive along length of wooden dowel. Wrap ribbon around dowel, stopping 1½ inches from end. Hold ends of red feathers along one side of unwrapped dowel. Continue wrapping ribbon around dowel securing ends of feathers inside ribbon. Secure with hot glue. Adhere dowel to mask base using hot glue.

Embellish mask with rhinestones.

Sources: *Die templates and die-cutting/embossing machine from Spellbinders™ Paper Arts; cardstock from American Crafts; patterned paper from Bo-Bunny Press; rhinestones and Creatology feathers from Michaels Stores Inc.*

Materials
Spellbinders™
- Nestabilities® die templates: (#S5-027) Labels Twenty-One, Grand Circles (#LF-114), Grand Scalloped Circles (#LF-124)
- Grand Calibur®

Additional
- Cardstock: black, white, cream
- Patterned papers: silver glitter dot metallic, Enchanted Love
- Black ink pad
- Black fine-tip marker
- Self-adhesive rhinestone flourishes
- Long red feathers
- 2 (⅞-inch-wide) 32-inch lengths silver glitter ribbon
- Blending tool
- Stapler
- Large adhesive dots
- Paper adhesive
- Strong double-sided adhesive
- Tape
- Computer with printer

Hat

Using #6 Grand Scalloped Circles die template, cut and emboss two scalloped circles, one from black cardstock and one from Enchanted Love paper.

Using #5 Grand Circles die template, cut and emboss a circle from silver glitter dot paper. Center and adhere to black scalloped circle.

Referring to photo and using strong double-sided adhesive, overlap and adhere one side of scalloped circles together; do not adhere outside edge of black scalloped circle down. Slightly overlap opposite edges of scalloped circles as shown; secure with a staple.

Referring to Reverse Stenciling technique, apply ink directly to outside edges of #3 Labels Twenty-One die template. Carefully position white cardstock over template; cut and emboss label.

Hand-print, or use computer to generate, "Happy New Year" onto cream cardstock. Referring to Die Cutting & Embossing Stamped Images technique, apply ink directly to outside edge of #2 Labels Twenty-One die template in the same manner as before. Cut and emboss a label around sentiment. Layer and adhere labels to front of hat as shown using adhesive dots.

Referring to photo, attach rhinestone flourishes to hat.

Cut a 9 x 4-inch piece of black cardstock. Cut fringe along one long edge of piece. Apply double-sided adhesive along one short edge and roll fringe piece into a tube; secure with tape. Insert feathers through center of tube and secure with tape. Curl cardstock fringe with fingers. Insert uncut end of fringed tube through top of hat. Secure with adhesive as needed.

Adhere two lengths of ribbon to inside of hat as shown as ties.

Sources: Die templates and die-cutting/embossing machine from Spellbinders™ Paper Arts; cardstock and glitter metallic paper from American Crafts; Enchanted Love paper from Bo-Bunny Press; rhinestones and Creatology feathers from Michaels Stores Inc.

Materials
Spellbinders™

- Nestabilities® Labels Twenty-One die templates (#S5-027)
- Shapeabilities® Ornate Artisan Tags and Accents die templates (#S5-070)
- Grand Calibur®

Additional

- Cardstock: black, white, red
- Enchanted Love patterned paper
- Small black gift bag
- Black ink pad
- Black feathers
- Ribbon: 1½-inch-wide black grosgrain, ⅞-inch-wide silver glitter
- Blending tool
- Black adhesive foam dots

Gift Bag

Cut a piece of patterned paper slightly smaller than front of gift bag. Referring to photo, layer and wrap silver and black ribbon around paper panel; secure ends to back. Adhere to bag front.

Referring to Making Frames technique and Reverse Stenciling technique, apply ink to #2 and #3 Labels Twenty-One die templates and cut a frame from white cardstock. Adhere to bag front as shown, using foam dots as desired.

Using Ornate Artisan Tags and Accents die template, cut and emboss flourishes from red cardstock. Adhere flourishes and feathers to bag front as shown.

Wrap silver ribbon around bag handle; tie a bow, and trim ends.

Sources: *Die templates and die-cutting/embossing machine from Spellbinders™ Paper Arts; cardstock from American Crafts; Enchanted Love paper from Bo-Bunny Press; rhinestones and Creatology feathers from Michaels Stores Inc.*

Card

From a 2¾ x 6-inch card from black cardstock. Referring to Making a Shaped Card technique and using #5 Labels Twenty-One die template, center die template onto black card and cut and emboss shaped card from card base. **Note:** *The card base is narrower than the die template—this creates an original shape.*

Using #4 Labels Twenty-One die template, cut and emboss a label from a 2¼ x 5-inch piece of patterned paper. Adhere to white cardstock, trim a small border. Adhere to card front.

Hand-print, or use computer to generate, sentiment onto white cardstock. Referring to Die Cutting & Embossing Stamped Images technique and Reverse Stenciling technique, apply ink directly to outside edge of #3 Labels Twenty-One die template. Cut and emboss a label around sentiment. Attach to card front using stacked foam squares. Embellish with rhinestones.

Adhere feathers to card front as shown. ■

Sources: *Die templates and die-cutting/embossing machine from Spellbinders™ Paper Arts; cardstock from American Crafts; patterned paper from Bo-Bunny Press; rhinestones and Creatology feathers from Michaels Stores Inc.*

Materials
Spellbinders™

- Nestabilities® Labels Twenty-One die templates (#S5-027)
- Grand Calibur®

Additional

- Cardstock: black, white
- Enchanted Harlequin patterned paper
- Black ink pad
- Black fine-tip marker
- Red self-adhesive rhinestones
- Feathers: black, red
- Blending tool
- Black adhesive foam squares
- Computer with printer

Happy Holidays

Holiday Gift Tags

DESIGNS BY **LESLEY LANGDON**

Paint tags with a wash of gesso paint; let dry.

Using Border Frosty Forms die template, emboss a fancy border across center of each shipping tag.

Adhere a length of mesh ribbon to each tag as shown. Apply adhesive along bottom sections of tags and sprinkle with glitter; let dry.

Using desired Frosty Forms die templates, cut and emboss shapes from patterned papers. Adhere to tags.

Cut lengths of twill with desired words; V-notch ends. Adhere twill sentiments and pearls to tags. Thread string through tag holes; tie knots and trim ends. ◼

Sources: *Die templates and die-cutting and embossing machine from Spellbinders™ Paper Arts; patterned papers from Lily Bee Design, My Mind's Eye and Melissa Frances; ribbon from Creative Impressions Inc.; self-adhesive pearls from Want2Scrap; glitter from Art Institute Glitter; Zip Dry quick-drying paper adhesive from Beacon Adhesives Inc.*

Materials
Spellbinders™
- Shapeabilities® Frosty Forms die templates (#S5-121)
- Grand Calibur®

Additional
- Various patterned papers
- Shipping tags
- White gesso paint
- Faux Snow glitter
- Ribbon: 2-inch-wide white mesh, ½-inch-wide various printed twill
- White self-adhesive pearls
- White string
- Paintbrush
- Quick-drying paper adhesive

Did You Know?
You can use sparkle glitter and pearls to dress the tags up.

Snowman & Reindeer Gift Set

DESIGNS BY **THERESA MOMBER**

Candy Holder

Using #5 Lacey Circles die template, cut and emboss a lacey circle from ivory cardstock. Using #7 Standard Circles LG die template, cut and emboss a circle from brown cardstock. Adhere circles together.

Using Accent Frosty Forms die templates, cut and emboss an accent shape from light brown cardstock; leave die template in place. Referring to Using Die Templates as Stencils technique, ink accent shape dark brown. Repeat six times for a total of seven inked accent pieces. Adhere accent shapes around outer edge of brown circle. This will be the candy holder base.

Cut a 3½ x 11-inch piece from ivory cardstock. Using Edger Classic Scallop and Three Petal Flower Classic Triple Scallop die templates nested together, cut and emboss one long edge of ivory piece; ink both long edges light brown using craft sponge. *Note: Secure nested dies together using painter's tape or repositionable tape as needed.*

With short edge of ivory piece horizontal on scoring board, score a vertical line ½ inch from uncut long edge, creating a ½-inch flap. Apply double-sided adhesive along outside edge of flap; remove lining. Cut slits into flap every ½ inch, creating ½-inch-wide tabs.

Form ivory piece into a tube and adhere ends together. *Note: If needed, cut a small section off decorative border edge where ends overlap so piece doesn't show through to front.* Fold in ½-inch tabs along bottom edge and adhere to candy-holder base as shown.

Using Border Frosty Forms die template, cut and emboss a border from light brown cardstock; leave die template in place and ink in the same manner as before. Repeat once for a total of two inked borders. Adhere around candy holder as shown.

Using Round Motif Frosty Forms die template, cut and emboss a motif from brown cardstock.

Using #1 Standard Circles SM die template, cut and emboss a circle from ivory

Materials
Spellbinders™
- Shapeabilities® Frosty Forms die templates (#S5-121)
- Nestabilities® die templates: Standard Circles LG (#S4-114), Standard Circles SM (#S4-116), Lacey Circles (#S4-293)
- Edgeabilities® die templates: Classic Scallop (#E8-001), Classic Triple Scallop (#E8-003)
- Grand Calibur®

Additional
- Cardstock: ivory, brown, light brown
- Small white sheer gift bag
- Chocolates
- Festive Frames stamp set
- Dye ink pads: light brown, dark brown
- Iridescent glitter pen
- Copic® markers: E31, W1
- Colorless Blender (0)
- Sheer ribbon: 16 inches ½-inch-wide brown patterned, 18 inches 1½-inch-wide brown, 17 inches ¾-inch-wide ivory
- Gold cord
- White self-adhesive pearls
- Scoring board
- Craft sponge
- Painter's tape or repositionable tape
- Adhesive foam squares
- Quick-drying paper adhesive
- Fabric adhesive
- Double-sided adhesive

cardstock; leave die template in place and add light brown ink in the same manner as before. Using dark brown ink, stamp "Joy" onto circle. Layer and adhere circle motif and sentiment circle to candy holder as shown, using foam squares.

Embellish candy holder with pearls.

Using Reindeer Frosty Forms die template, cut and emboss a reindeer from ivory cardstock; leave die template in place and add light brown ink in the same manner as before. Color reindeer with markers and Colorless Blender.

In the same manner, cut another reindeer from light brown cardstock. Color only the antlers with glitter pen. Cut off antlers from light brown reindeer and glue on top of antlers on ivory reindeer. Tie a short length of gold cord in a bow around reindeer's neck.

Materials
Spellbinders™
- Shapeabilities® die templates: Frosty Forms (#S5-121), Tags and Flags (#S5-095), Labels and Tags (#S5-094)
- Nestabilities® die templates: Labels Twenty-Eight (#S5-127), Labels and Tags (#S5-094)
- Grand Calibur®

Additional
- Cardstock: ivory, brown, light brown
- Wishing You Joy stamp set
- Dye ink pads: light brown, dark brown
- Dye ink markers: orange, dark brown
- Copic® markers: E31, W1
- Colorless Blender (0)
- Iridescent glitter pen
- Gold cord
- Sheer ¾-inch-wide ribbon: 14 inches brown, 14 inches ivory
- White self-adhesive pearls
- Copper eyelet with ¼-inch hole
- Hole punches: ¼-inch, ⅛-inch
- Eyelet setting tool
- Craft sponge
- Adhesive foam squares
- Quick-drying paper adhesive
- Double-sided adhesive

Fill gift bag with chocolates. Tie a bow with each length of ribbon; trim ends. Lay bows on top of each other, wrap long length of gold cord around middle of bows; tie knot on back to secure bows together. Wrap cord around top of bag; tie bow, trim ends. Adhere reindeer to center of layered bow using fabric glue. Place bag into candy holder.

Sources: Die templates and die-cutting/embossing machine from Spellbinders™ Paper Arts; cardstock and stamp set from Gina K. Designs; Memento ink pads from Imagine Crafts/Tsukineko; glitter pen from Sakura of America; markers and Colorless Blender from Copic®/Imagination International Inc.; ribbon from Creative Impressions Inc.; self-adhesive pearls from Want2Scrap; Scor-Pal scoring board and double-sided adhesive from Scor-Pal Products; foam squares from SCRAPBOOK ADHESIVES BY 3L™; Zip Dry quick-drying paper adhesive and Fabric-Tac fabric adhesive from Beacon Adhesives Inc.

Gift Tag

Using Tags and Flags die template, cut and emboss a tag from ivory cardstock; leave die template in place. Referring to Using a Die Template as Stencils technique, ink tag light brown. Punch a ¼-inch hole through top of tag. Using eyelet-setting tool, set copper eyelet in hole.

Using Round Motif Frosty Forms die template, cut and emboss two motifs from dark brown cardstock. Attach to tag as shown using foam squares.

Using 3 x 1½-inch Labels and Tags die template, cut and emboss a label from light brown cardstock; leave die template in place and add dark brown ink in the same manner as before. Holding both lengths of ribbon together, wrap ribbon around label; tie bow and trim ends. Attach label to tag using foam squares.

Using Snowman Frosty Forms die template, cut and emboss a snowman from ivory cardstock; leave die template in place and add light brown ink in the same manner as before. Use dye markers to draw snowman's face; add subtle color to snowman with Copic markers and Colorless Blender.

Did You Know?

These same projects can be created in traditional Christmas colors, or cool blues and whites for a wintery look.

Using Fancy Ribbon Frosty Forms die template, cut and emboss a fancy ribbon from light brown cardstock; leave die template in place and add dark brown ink in the same manner as before. Color inked section of fancy ribbon with glitter pen. Adhere to snowman. Attach snowman to tag with foam squares.

Using #1 Labels Twenty-Eight die template, cut and emboss a label from ivory cardstock; leave die template in place and add light brown ink in the same manner as before. Stamp "To:" and "From:" onto label with dark

brown ink. Punch a ⅛-inch hole through label as shown. Thread a short length of gold cord through hole, wrap around ribbon on tag and tie knot; trim ends. Secure label with adhesive as desired.

Embellish tag with pearls as desired. ■

Sources: *Die templates and die-cutting/embossing machine from Spellbinders™ Paper Arts; cardstock and stamp set from Gina K. Designs; Memento ink pads and markers from Imagine Crafts/Tsukineko; glitter pen from Sakura of America; markers and Colorless Blender from Copic®/Imagination International Inc.; ribbon from Creative Impressions Inc.; self-adhesive pearls from Want2Scrap; double-sided adhesive from Scor-Pal Products; foam squares from SCRAPBOOK ADHESIVES BY 3L™; Zip Dry quick-drying paper adhesive from Beacon Adhesives Inc.*

Etched Elegance

DESIGN BY **DARSIE BRUNO**

Project note: Plate is for display purposes only. **Do not use for serving food.**

Thoroughly wash and dry glass plate and set aside.

Using Tree 2012 Holiday Tree die template, cut a tree from self-adhesive vinyl.

Using Border Frosty Forms die template, cut four borders from self-adhesive vinyl. Cut four Accents from self-adhesive vinyl.

Peel off protective backing from tree die cut; place die cut onto center of glass plate. With squeegee, firmly rub vinyl until all air bubbles are removed and tree stencil is flat against plate. **Note:** *This is an important step to keep the etching creme from seeping underneath the vinyl stencil.* In the same manner and referring to photo, attach vinyl accents and borders to plate.

Liberally apply etching creme onto plate with squeegee. **Note:** *Don't be afraid to use all of the creme. Once the etching is finished, the excess creme can be put back into the jar to use again.* Wait 15 minutes for glass to etch.

Use squeegee to remove creme and put it back into jar. Be careful not to dislodge the vinyl stencils.

Once most of the creme is removed, submerge plate into bucket of water. Remove rest of creme with sponge. The vinyl pieces may come off during this process, but it is OK.

Remove all vinyl pieces, rinse plate again and then dry with a towel. The etched surface will appear once your plate is dry.

Wrap a 27-inch length of red silk ribbon around plate; tie a bow, V-notch ends.

Cut remaining red silk ribbon into two 6-inch lengths. Fold one length in half, creating a loop; secure loop with a drop of glue and let dry. Repeat with other 6-inch ribbon length. Add drop of glue to edges of loops and insert them between bow loops, creating the appearance of a double bow. Let dry.

Using #3 and #2 2012 Heirloom Ornaments die templates, cut and emboss two ornaments from desired patterned papers. Using black ink, stamp sentiment and snowflakes onto smaller ornament.

Using Accent Frosty Forms die template, cut and emboss three accents from gold metallic paper. Referring to photo, layer and adhere ornaments and accents together using foam dots as desired.

Materials
Spellbinders™
- Shapeabilities® die templates: 2012 Holiday Tree (#S4-339), Frosty Forms (#S5-121)
- Nestabilities® 2012 Heirloom Ornaments die templates (#S5-116)
- Grand Calibur®

Additional
- Square glass plate
- Various holiday-themed paper
- Gold metallic paper
- Self-adhesive vinyl
- Etching creme
- Winter Words stamp set
- Black dye ink pad
- Copic® marker: YG63
- Ribbon: 39 inches 1¼-inch-wide red silk, 6 inches ⅛-inch-wide cream
- Gold self-adhesive pearls
- ⅛-inch hole punch
- Bucket of water
- Sponge
- Towel
- Polyethylene squeegee
- Adhesive foam dots
- Craft glue

Punch a hole through top of layered ornaments. Wrap cream ribbon around bow on plate; thread ribbon through hole and tie bow, trim ends.

Embellish plate with pearls as desired. ■

Sources: *Die templates and die-cutting/embossing machine from Spellbinders™ Paper Arts; etching creme from Etchall; stamp set from JustRite; Memento ink pad from Imagine Crafts/Tsukineko; marker from Copic®/Imagination International Inc.; ribbon from May Arts; self-adhesive pearls from Michaels Stores Inc.; foam dots from SCRAPBOOK ADHESIVES BY 3L™; 3-in-1 craft glue from Beacon Adhesives Inc.*

Home Decor

Pretty Vellum Vase Wrap

DESIGN BY **KIMBERLY CRAWFORD**

Cut three 4 x 12-inch pieces from vellum.

Referring to Extending Embossed Areas technique and using embossing folder, emboss each piece of vellum.

Apply adhesive to one end of a piece of vellum; wrap vellum around candle holder and adhere ends together. Wrap a length of ribbon around candle holder over vellum; tie bow and V-notch ends. Repeat with remaining candle holders. ■

Sources: Embossing folder and die-cutting/embossing machine from Spellbinders™ Paper Arts; vellum from WorldWin Papers; candle holders and ribbon from Michaels Stores Inc.; vellum adhesive from SCRAPBOOK ADHESIVES BY 3L™.

Materials
Spellbinders™
- M-Bossabilities™ Paisley embossing folder (#EL-010)
- Grand Calibur®

Additional
- 3 clear glass tumbler-style candle holders
- Vellum
- 1½-inch-wide wire-edged satin ribbon in desired colors
- Double-sided vellum adhesive

Embossed Foil Frame

DESIGN BY **WINDY ROBINSON**

Materials
Spellbinders™
- Craft Foil Assortments: Precious Metals Premium (#F-012), Jewel Tones Premium (#F-013)
- Shapeabilities® Bitty Blossoms die templates (#S5-086)
- Nestabilities® die templates: Classic Squares LG (#S4-126), Classic Squares SM (#S4-128)
- M-Bossabilities™ Paisley embossing folder (#EL-010)
- Grand Calibur®

Additional
- Kraft cardstock
- Real Wood Birch Paper sheet
- 8 x 8-inch wood panel frame
- Dark brown chalk ink pad
- Clear self-adhesive gems
- Sanding block
- Blending tool
- Hot-glue gun
- Adhesive foam dots
- Craft glue

Did You Know?
You should allow frame to thoroughly dry before sanding to avoid shifting of metal panels.

Using #6 Classic Squares LG die template, cut eight squares from three different colors of craft foil. Emboss squares using Paisley embossing folder, alternating between both embossing folders in set.

Referring to photo, adhere foil squares to frame. Fold and adhere edges of overhanging foil pieces to sides of frame. Referring to Sanding Embossed Areas technique, sand surface.

Using #6 Classic Squares SM die template, cut a square from photo. Using #6 Classic Squares LG die template, cut a square from silver craft foil. Using #7 Classic Squares SM die template, cut a square from birch wood sheet. Layer and adhere squares together. Attach to center of frame using foam dots.

Using Flower LG and Flower SM Bitty Blossoms die templates, cut and emboss one large flower and two small flowers from kraft cardstock. Referring to Making a Spiral Flower technique, roll and assemble flowers with hot glue.

Using Double Leaves Bitty Blossoms die template, cut and emboss double leaves from kraft cardstock; leave die template in place. Referring to Using Die Templates as Stencils technique, ink leaves brown. Remove die template.

Layer and adhere leaves and flowers to frame with hot glue. Embellish flowers with gems. ■

Sources: Craft foil, die templates, embossing folder and die-cutting/embossing machine from Spellbinders™ Paper Arts; cardstock from Bazzill Basics Paper Inc.; birch paper from Creative Imaginations; frame from Walnut Hollow; chalk ink pad from Clearsnap Inc.; self-adhesive gems from Want2Scrap; Sand It Gadget from Core'dinations; 3-in-1 craft glue from Beacon Adhesives Inc.

Timeless Treasures Box

DESIGN BY **CATHY CHLEBANA**

Materials
Spellbinders™
- M-Bossabilities™ Paisley embossing folder (#EL-010)
- Grand Calibur®

Additional
- Card Keeper Box
- Copper Pure Metal Tooling Foil 36 gauge
- Black acrylic paint
- Dark brown acrylic medium
- Liver of sulfur
- 4 decorative metal box feet
- Paintbrushes
- Palette knife
- Sanding block
- Painter's tape
- All-purpose permanent adhesive

Paint box, box lid and inside of box with black paint. Let dry completely.

Cut five 5 x 7-inch pieces from copper foil. Emboss foil pieces using embossing folders. **Note:** *Example was embossed as follows: three pieces with side A and two pieces with side B.*

Following manufacturer's instructions and working in a well-ventilated area or outdoors, prepare liver of sulfur solution and place embossed copper pieces into solution to give pieces a patina. Remove copper pieces from solution; let dry. Referring to Sanding Embossed Areas technique and using sanding block, remove patina finish on embossed areas to highlight design.

Referring to photo, trim embossed pieces to fit box top and sides. Adhere pieces to box; hold pieces in place using painter's tape until adhesive dries.

Using a palette knife, liberally apply dark brown acrylic medium to corners and edges of box for added texture. Let dry.

When paint has dried, adhere box feet to bottom corners of box. Let dry. ■

Sources: *Embossing folder and die-cutting/embossing machine from Spellbinders™ Paper Arts; Card Keeper Box from Walnut Hollow; Pure Metal Tooling Foil from Dick Blick Art Materials; Ferro dark brown acrylic medium from Viva Décor; Tim Holtz Findings Foundations Box Feet from Ranger Industries Inc.; Quick Grip all-purpose permanent adhesive from Beacon Adhesives Inc.*

Jewelry

Romantic Roses

DESIGNS BY **CHRISTINE EMBERSON**

Romantic Roses Pendant

Using Circle Tag Fancy Framed Tags Two die template, cut and emboss two circle tags from desired color of craft foil. Referring to photo, use Circle Tag Insert die template to cut out centers of circle tags. To reinforce the foil, apply a layer of adhesive on back sides of circle openings only. Let dry completely. Do not adhere tags together.

Referring to photo, slide three beads onto head pin. Using round-nose pliers and referring to Creating a Simple Loop technique, create a small loop on beaded head pin. **Note:** *Secure beads in place on head pin with adhesive if desired.*

Thread a crimp bead, beaded head pin and a crimp bead onto circular ear wire, positioning head pin so it dangles inside the circular ear wire. Secure beaded head pin in place by flattening crimp beads with flat-nose pliers. Cut off small loop from ear wire.

Sandwich ear wire with beaded dangle between foil circle tags and adhere in place, making sure sides of circle tags are adhered together. Let dry.

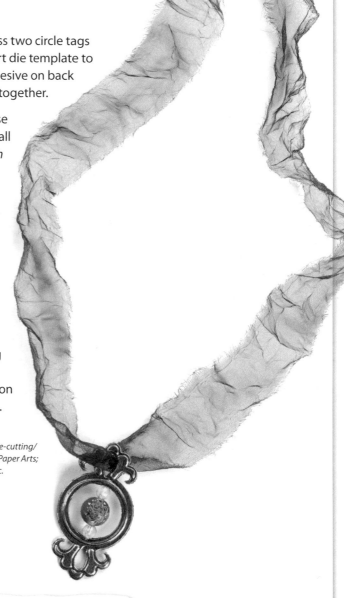

Thread ribbon through top hole of circle tag, sliding tag to center of ribbon. Thread ribbon ends through loops on clasp and secure with knots. Trim excess ribbon.

Sources: Craft foils, die templates and die-cutting/ embossing machine from Spellbinders™ Paper Arts; Glossy Accents from Ranger Industries Inc.

Materials
Spellbinders™
- Precious Metals Premium Craft Foils Assortment (#F-012)
- Shapeabilities® Fancy Frames Tags Two die templates (#S5-128)
- Grand Calibur®

Additional
- 26 inches 1-inch-wide brown sheer ribbon
- Round glass beads: 1 large, 2 medium, 2 crimp beads
- Head pin
- 1-inch circular ear wire
- Barrel clasp
- Round-nose pliers
- Flat-nose pliers
- Wire cutters
- Glossy Accents™ adhesive

Did You Know?
For a different look, slide pendant onto a necklace chain instead of ribbon.

Romantic Roses Gift Card

Form a 4 x 4⅞-inch card from cream cardstock.

Cut a 3¾ x 4¾-inch piece from Waltz paper. Wrap ribbon around paper as shown; secure ends to back. Adhere to card front.

Using Oval Tag LG Fancy Framed Tags Two die template, cut and emboss an oval tag from Reunion paper. Using Circle Tag die template, cut and emboss a circle tag from desired color of craft foil. Using Circle Tag Insert die template, cut a circle insert from Reunion paper.

Referring to photo and using foam squares, layer and attach die-cut pieces to card front.

Stamp sentiment onto solid side of Waltz paper. Referring to Die Cutting & Embossing Stamped Images technique and using Oval Tag LG Insert die template, cut and emboss an oval around sentiment. Attach to card front as shown, using foam squares. ■

Sources: *Craft foils, die templates and die-cutting/embossing machine from Spellbinders™ Paper Arts; patterned papers from Kaisercraft; stamp set from Gina K. Designs; self-adhesive pearls from Want2Scrap; double-sided tape from SCRAPBOOK ADHESIVES BY 3L™.*

Materials
Spellbinders™
- Precious Metals Premium Craft Foils Assortment (#F-012)
- Shapeabilities® Fancy Frames Tags Two die templates (#S5-128)
- Grand Calibur®

Additional
- Cream cardstock
- Patterned papers: These Days Reunion, After Five Waltz
- Labeled with Love stamp set
- Brown dye ink pad
- 6 inches ⅜-inch-wide brown/white dot ribbon
- Cream self-adhesive pearls
- Adhesive foam squares
- Double-sided tape

Did You Know?
Using different colors of craft foils and beads creates an array of beaded Fancy Frame pendants.

Sparkling Turquoise Earrings & Card

DESIGNS BY **HEIDI BLANKENSHIP**

Earrings

Using Oval Tag LG Fancy Framed Tags Two die template, cut two oval tags from clear shrink plastic. Using Oval Tag LG Insert die template, cut two oval inserts from black shrink plastic.

Stamp a flourish onto each black shrink plastic oval insert. Let dry completely.

Place shrink plastic die-cut pieces onto a piece of parchment paper and bake in oven according to manufacturer's instructions. After baking, remove from oven and let cool completely.

Use airbrush system and marker to apply color to clear oval tags; let dry.

Using Glossy Accents, adhere black ovals to colored oval tags. In the same manner, adhere rhinestones to black ovals. Apply a coat of Glossy Accents on top of the black ovals; set aside to dry.

Thread amethyst bead, bead cap and bicone bead onto a head pin. Referring to Creating a Simple Loop technique, create a loop at top of beaded head pin. Repeat with a second head pin.

Referring to How to Open & Close a Jump Ring technique, open a jump ring and connect beaded head pin to bottom of oval tag. Close jump ring. In the same manner, open a jump ring and slide on top of oval tag and another jump ring; close ring. In the same manner, open loop on bottom of ear wire and slide top jump ring onto ear wire loop; close loop. Repeat to create second earring.

Sources: *Die templates and die-cutting/embossing machine from Spellbinders™ Paper Arts; Glossy Accents from Ranger Industries Inc.; shrink plastic from Shrinky Dinks®; stamp set from JustRite; StazOn solvent ink pad from Imagine Crafts/Tsukineko; marker and airbrush system from Copic®/Imagination International Inc.; Diamond & Pearls flat-back rhinestones from The Rubber Café; tape from 3M.*

Materials
Spellbinders™
- Shapeabilities® Fancy Frames Tags Two die templates (#S5-128)
- Grand Calibur®

Additional
- Shrink plastic: clear, black
- Botanical Medallions & Banners stamp set
- Silver metallic solvent ink pad
- Copic® marker: B04
- Small clear flat-back rhinestones
- Crystal beads: 2 (4mm) blue bicone, 2 (6mm) amethyst teardrop
- 2 (6mm) silver decorative bead caps
- 2 silver French ear wires
- 2 (1-inch) silver head pins
- 6 (6mm) silver jump rings
- Parchment paper
- Oven
- Rhinestone setter
- Round-nose pliers
- Needle-nose pliers
- Wire cutters
- Copic® airbrush system
- Glossy Accents™ adhesive
- Tape (optional)

Card

Form a 6½ x 5½-inch card from black cardstock. Referring to Making a Shaped Card technique and using #4 Decorative Labels Eight die template, cut and emboss a shaped card from card base.

Materials
Spellbinders™
- Precious Metals Premium Craft Foils Assortment (#F-012)
- Nestabilities® die templates: Decorative Labels Eight (#S5-148), Resplendent Rectangles (#S5-147)
- Shapeabilities® Fancy Framed Tags Two die templates (#S5-128)
- Grand Calibur®

Additional
- Cardstock: white smooth, black
- Stamp sets: Botanical Medallions & Banners, Just Because Vintage Labels
- Ink pads: silver metallic solvent, black dye
- Copic® marker: B04
- Small clear flat-back rhinestones
- Silver round filigrees: 1 small, 1 medium
- 18 inches ⅜-inch-wide white dot sheer ribbon
- Baby powder
- Copic® airbrush system
- Paintbrush
- Hot-glue gun
- Repositionable tape
- Adhesive foam squares
- Double-sided adhesive sheet
- Multi-purpose craft glue

Apply adhesive sheet to a 6½ x 5½-inch piece of black cardstock. Cut and emboss a #4 Decorative Labels Eight label from adhesive-backed black cardstock. Remove backing from adhesive sheet and adhere to card front, aligning bottom and side edges. ***Note:*** *To remove stickiness on back of card from adhesive, dust with baby powder and use a paintbrush to remove excess powder.*

Using #4 Resplendent Rectangles die template, cut and emboss a rectangle from white cardstock; leave die template in place. Referring to Using Die Templates as Stencils technique, ink die cut using marker and airbrush system; leave die template in place. Stamp flourish onto die cut with silver metallic ink. Remove die template.

Using Oval Tag LG Fancy Framed Tags Two die template, cut and emboss an oval tag from silver craft foil. Using Oval Tag LG Insert die template, cut and emboss an oval insert from white cardstock; leave die template in place. Airbrush color onto oval insert in the same manner as before. Stamp sentiment onto oval insert with black ink.

Layer and attach die cuts to card front as shown, using foam squares as desired.

Using rhinestone setting tool and clear-drying liquid adhesive, embellish card front with flat-back rhinestones.

Tie a multi-loop bow with ribbon; trim ends. Using hot glue, layer and attach bow and round filigrees to card front as shown. Attach a rhinestone to center of filigree in the same manner as before. ◼

Sources: Craft foil, die templates and die-cutting/embossing machine from Spellbinders™ Paper Arts; stamp sets from JustRite; StazOn solvent ink pad and Memento dye ink pad from Imagine Crafts/Tsukineko; marker and airbrush system from Copic®/Imagination International Inc.; ribbon from Really Reasonable Ribbon; foam squares and double-sided adhesive sheet from SCRAPBOOK ADHESIVES BY 3L™; Scrap Happy Sheer Glue (multi-purpose craft glue) from The Rubber Café.

Did You Know?
The Stick "EM" Up Tool can be used for perfect placement of loose rhinestones.

Spellbound Beauty Necklace

DESIGN BY **JEN CUSHMAN**

Using Oval Tag LG Fancy Framed Tags Two die template, cut an oval tag from chipboard. Repeat, cutting an oval tag from vintage sheet music. Adhere oval tags together with resin by putting resin on tags and layering them on top of each other.

Apply watermark ink to oval tag; sprinkle with a mix of both copper and verdigris embossing powders, heat-emboss. **Note:** *Try covering just sections of tag with embossing enamel to give tag a distressed look.*

Using Oval Tag LG Insert Fancy Framed Tags Two die template, cut image from collage paper to fit inside of medium bezel.

Apply paper sealer onto die-cut collage image; let dry. Place dry, sealed image inside bezel. **Note:** *Using a paper sealer on your image ensures that the image colors will not bleed when resin is applied over it.*

Following manufacturer's instructions, mix enough resin to fill bezel. Pour mixed resin into bezel filling the bezel up halfway. Sprinkle glitter into half-filled bezel as desired. Pour remaining resin into bezel until it is full. Let dry thoroughly, approximately 6–10 hours.

When bezel is dry to the touch, mix up a little more resin. To adhere bezel to oval tag, place resin onto center of tag and place bezel onto resin. Add a length of rhinestone chain around outside of bezel and two flat-back crystals above and below bezel, pressing them into the resin. Let resin dry completely, approximately 6–10 hours. **Note:** *Resin will be more secure than using glue to adhere components to oval tag.*

Referring to Creating a Wrapped Loop Link technique, create a wrapped loop link from a 4-inch piece of wire, connecting one end of link to top of oval tag before finishing wrap.

Materials
Spellbinders™
- Shapeabilities® Fancy Framed Tags Two die templates (#S5-128)
- Grand Calibur®

Additional
- Oval Hobnail bronze Bezel medium (#SLK905BP)
- Chipboard
- Art Mechanique Belles Dames Francaise Flip Book (collage images)
- Vintage sheet music
- Watermark ink pad
- Top Boss embossing powders: copper, verdigris
- Cirque Glass Glitter set
- Rondelles: 1 light brown crystal, 1 silver with clear rhinestones
- 2 flat-back crystals
- Art Mechanique™ 20-gauge bronze wire
- Susan Lenart Kazmer Industrial Chic™ chain: bronze necklace, rhinestone
- Bonze jump rings: 1 decorative oval, 2 large round
- Bronze large lobster-claw clasp
- 2-inch bronze ball-tipped head pin
- Embossing heat tool
- Round-nose pliers
- Wire cutters
- Art Mechanique paper sealer
- Clear self-doming resin

Referring to How to Create a Wrapped Loop Dangle technique, create a dangle using ball-tipped head pin, crystal rondelle and silver rondelle. Connect dangle to bottom of oval tag before finishing wrap.

Cut two 17-inch lengths of chain. Lay chains on work surface next to each other and locate center links. Referring to How to Open & Close a Jump Ring technique, open an oval jump ring and thread it through both center links of chains and through top loop of wrapped link. Close jump loop.

Open a round jump ring, thread end links of both chains on one side of necklace onto jump ring. Close ring. Open another round jump ring, thread on lobster-claw clasp and remaining ends of chains; close ring. ■

Sources: *Die templates and die-cutting/embossing machine from Spellbinders™ Paper Arts; Hobnail Bezel, flip book, glass glitter, wire, chains, paper sealer and Ice Resin® from ICE Resin; watermark ink pad from Imagine Crafts/Tsukineko; embossing powders from Clearsnap Inc.*

Did You Know?

For a nice dome, drip resin with a craft stick drip by drip until dome forms. Be careful not to overfill.

Mixed Media

Baby Keepsake Box

DESIGN BY **SHERRY CHEEVER**

Project note: *Ink edges and die-cut edges of all patterned paper pieces light brown. Use pieces of foam sheet to apply ink.*

Paint both outside and inside of box with two coats of off-white acrylic paint; let dry.

Cut the following: three 5 x 5-inch pieces and two 5 x 1⅜-inch strips from Peek-A-Boo paper, and two 5 x 5-inch pieces, one 4¾ x 4¾-inch piece and two 5 x 1⅜-inch strips from Heaven Sent paper.

Using #6 Classic Squares LG die template, cut a square opening from center of a 5 x 5-inch piece of Peek-A-Boo paper, creating a frame. Repeat with a 5 x 5-inch piece of Heaven Sent paper.

Materials

Spellbinders™
- Nestabilities® die templates: Labels Twenty-Seven (#S4-376), Classic Squares LG (#S4-126)
- Grand Calibur®

Additional
- 5 x 5-inch kraft board altered art box
- Cream cardstock
- Little Darlings patterned papers: Peek-A-Boo, Heaven Sent
- Little Darlings Chipboard die cuts: 1, 2
- Light brown distress ink pad
- Off-white acrylic paint
- Metal button
- Metal tag
- Ivory ribbon: 14 inches 1-inch-wide satin stitched, 12 inches ½-inch-wide seam binding
- Rattle Favor Accent (#1103-29)
- Self-adhesive magnets
- Foam sheet
- Soft cloth
- Paintbrushes
- Blending tool
- Glossy Accents™ adhesive
- Matte multi-medium art gel
- Hot-glue gun (medium temperature)
- Adhesive foam tape

Determine placement for magnet on inside of front flap; attach magnet in place. Adhere other half of magnet onto inside cover of box, aligning it with magnet on inside of front flap. **Note:** *This will typically be over the magnet provided in the box. This is necessary because of the additional paint and paper that will be added.*

Referring to photo and using multi-medium art gel, adhere patterned papers to box.

Using Labels Twenty-Seven die templates, cut and emboss a #4 label from Peek-A-Boo paper and a #3 label and a #4 label from Heaven Sent paper. Set aside.

Referring to Using Die Templates as Stencils technique and using Labels Twenty-Seven die templates, cut, emboss and stencil two #5 labels and one #3 label from cream cardstock.

Layer and adhere the following labels together: #3 Heaven Sent, #4 Peek-A-Boo and #5 cream. Repeat with #3 cream label, #4 Heaven Sent label and #5 cream label.

Ink edges of following chipboard die cuts: "For Baby" tag, baby flower and button. Cut a 6-inch length from seam binding and thread it through chipboard button; tie bow on front, trim ends. Adhere to first set of layered labels. Adhere to back of inside box flap.

Adhere baby flower chipboard piece to center of second set of layered labels; adhere to inside flap of box so chipboard flower shows through front opening.

Paint back of "For Baby" tag with acrylic paint; let dry. Thread remaining length of seam binding through tag and rattle; tie bow, trim ends. Thread satin stiched ribbon through rattle and tag; tie bow, trim ends. Attach to box front as shown using foam tape.

Paint metal tag and button with acrylic paint; let dry. When dry remove some paint with a wet cloth. Adhere tag and button to box front as shown using hot glue. ◼

Sources: *Die templates and die-cutting/embossing machine from Spellbinders™ Paper Arts; cardstock from Stampin' Up!; patterned papers, chipboard die cuts, art box, metal button and tag from Graphic 45; Cut n' Dry foam sheet, distress ink pad, Claudine Hellmuth Studio matte multi-medium art gel and Glossy Accents from Ranger Industries Inc.; ribbon from May Arts; rattle from Wilton Industries; self-adhesive magnets from BasicGrey.*

The Times of Our Lives Canvas

DESIGN BY **KEN OLIVER**

Materials
Spellbinders™
- Precious Metals Premium Craft Foils Assortment (#F-012)
- Nestabilities® die templates: Labels Twenty-Seven (#S4-376), Grand Rectangles (#LF-132) Grand Labels Four (#LF-190)
- Shapeabilities® die templates: Bitty Blossoms (#S5-086), Bauble Blossom One (#S5-103)
- M-Bossabilites™ Nobility embossing folder (#ES-002)
- Grand Calibur®

Additional
- 8 x 10-inch canvas
- Cardstock: kraft, copper metallic
- Vintage family photos
- Chipboard
- Handwritten text stamp
- Chalk ink pads: dark brown, dark blue
- Acrylic paints: blue, rust brown, green
- Clockface
- Assorted metal accessories including key, charm, brass plate, button, wires, assorted ribbons
- Stipple brush
- Paintbrush
- Quilling tool
- Extra-fine sandpaper
- Matte decoupage medium
- Liquid adhesive
- Industrial-strength craft adhesive

Using dark blue ink, stamp entire canvas with handwritten text. Ink edges of canvas dark brown.

Cut a 6¼ x 6¼-inch piece from kraft cardstock; round corners with scissors. Using dark blue ink, stamp handwritten text onto piece. Ink edges dark brown.

Using #2 Grand Labels Four die template, cut and emboss a label from kraft cardstock. Set aside.

Using #4 and #3 Labels Twenty-Seven die templates and referring to Making Frames technique, cut and emboss a frame from copper cardstock. Repeat using #5 and #3 die templates. Stipple brown, blue and green paint onto frames. Let dry.

Using Flower LG Bitty Blossoms die template, cut and emboss a flower from copper cardstock. Cut and emboss Double Leaves from copper cardstock. Referring to Making a Spiral Flower technique, roll and assemble flower. Stipple die cuts with blue paint; let dry. Set aside.

Using Nobility embossing folder, emboss a 3 x 3-inch piece of gold craft foil. Stipple with brown and blue paint; let dry. Trim one embossed rectangle from embossed sheet. Adhere to metal charm. Thread a scrap piece of ribbon through charm; tie knot, trim ends.

Using #3 Grand Rectangles die template, cut and emboss a rectangle from copper cardstock. Paint with blue and brown paints as desired; let dry.

Paint metal accessories as desired; let dry.

Layer and adhere die cuts, photos and assorted metal accessories onto canvas as desired saving metal button for clockface. Use liquid adhesive to adhere cardstock pieces and craft adhesive to adhere metal pieces.

To assemble clockface, first cut a ⅜-inch-wide strip of kraft cardstock long enough to fit diameter of clockface. Form cardstock strip into a circle matching clockface's diameter. Apply a coat of decoupage medium onto cardstock circle; let dry. Use liquid adhesive to adhere circle to back of clockface; let dry completely. Apply another layer of decoupage medium onto cardstock circle helping to secure it to clockface. Hand-cut clock hands from chipboard; ink dark brown. Adhere clock hands and metal button to clockface. Wrap ribbon around side of clock. Adhere clockface to canvas.

Using Quilling Strip Bauble Blossom One die template, cut four quilling strips from kraft cardstock; ink dark brown. Using quilling tool, roll each quilling strip into a **S Scroll** (see illustration). Adhere shapes to canvas.

S Scroll

Apply a thin coat of decoupage medium to entire surface of canvas. Let dry completely.

When dry, lightly sand with sandpaper, and ink edges and crevices dark brown. Apply another thin coat of decoupage medium; let dry. ■

Sources: Die templates and die-cutting/embossing machine from Spellbinders™ Paper Arts Inc.; canvas and copper metallic cardstock from Michaels Stores Inc.; craft foil, Time Flies Kraft Clocks clockface from Maya Road; chalk ink pads from Quick Quotes.

Materials
Spellbinders™
- Nestabilities® die templates: Labels Twenty-Seven (#S4-376), Fleur de Lis Rectangles (#S4-317)
- Shapeabilities® die templates: Ribbon Banners (#S4-324), Bitty Blossoms (#S5-086)
- Grand Calibur®

Additional
- Cardstock: white, red
- Patterned papers: Mistables 12 x 12-inch paper pack, assorted patterned papers
- Photos
- Lucky to Have You (KOM 2/12) stamp set
- Ink pads: blue chalk, green chalk, brown solvent, black solvent
- Sheer ink sprays: teal, green, yellow
- Glimmer ink sprays: teal, peach
- Heart Hobnail silver-plated Bezel medium (#SLK917SP)
- Bronze brad
- Self-adhesive gems
- 12 inches ¾-inch-wide white polka dot sheer ribbon
- Decorative stickpins
- Silver crushed glass glitter
- Clear self-doming resin
- Adhesive tape runner
- Liquid paper adhesive

Lucky to Have You Album

DESIGN BY **HOLLY SIMONI**

Using #5 Labels Twenty-Seven die template, cut and emboss one label from desired Mistables paper and seven from desired patterned papers. ***Note:*** *If more pages are desired, cut and emboss additional labels, cutting two labels for each additional page.* Ink labels as desired. Add more color to pages with sheer and glimmer ink sprays. Let dry.

Ink Mistables label with chalk ink blending blue and green inks together. Let dry.

Adhere a patterned paper label to back of Mistables label, creating base for front cover. Adhere two paper labels together to create a page. Repeat for each page. Using brown ink, stamp "LUCKY TO HAVE YOU" onto white cardstock. Referring to Die Cutting & Embossing Stamped Images technique and using #3 Ribbon Banners die template, cut and emboss a banner around sentiment. Ink edges blue. Referring to photo, adhere ends of sentiment banner to front cover of album; curve slightly with fingers to add dimension before adhering. Embellish with gems and stickpins as shown; secure stickpins in place using paper adhesive.

Using desired-size Bitty Blossoms Flower die template and referring to Making a Spiral Flower technique, cut a flower from red cardstock. Roll and assemble flower following manufacturer's instructions. Set aside.

Cut out desired elements that will be placed inside heart bezel from patterned papers. Trace heart bezel onto desired patterned paper; cut out heart. Place paper heart and paper elements into bezel heart. **Note:** *If using an element like a butterfly, try folding butterfly's wings upward so its wings will be lifted up in bezel.*

Following manufacturer's instructions, mix enough resin to fill bezel. Fill bezel half full with mixed resin. Place rolled flower into bezel, pressing it gently into resin. Sprinkle glitter into bezel and on flower as desired. Fill bezel with remaining resin, allowing some resin to pour over rolled flower. Let dry thoroughly, approximately 6–10 hours.

When dry, mix a small amount of resin in the same manner as before. Spread resin onto front cover where bezel will be adhered and press bezel into resin. Let dry thoroughly.

Referring to Die Cutting & Embossing Stamped Images technique and using #3 Fleur de Lis Rectangle die template, cut and emboss desired section of photo. Adhere to back cover of album.

Decorate inside pages as desired.

Stack album pages together, wrap ribbon around pages; tie knot, trim ends. ■

Sources: Die templates and die-cutting/embossing machine from Spellbinders™ Paper Arts; cardstock from WorldWin Papers; Mistables paper pack from Pink Paislee; chalk ink pads from Clearsnap Inc.; StazOn solvent ink pads from Imagine Crafts/Tsukineko; Plain Jane Simply Sheer Mists and Glimmer Mists from Tattered Angels; Hobnail Bezel and self-doming resin from ICE Resin®; self-adhesive gems from Want2Scrap; ribbon from Maya Road; stickpins from Little Yellow Bicycle; glass glitter from Stampendous! Inc.; adhesive tape runner from 3M.

Inside Page Materials
Spellbinders™
- Nestabilities® die templates: Wonderful Wings (#LF-006), Postage Stamps (#S4-348)
- Shapeabilities® die templates: Fancy Tags Three (#S5-031), Labels and Tags (#S5-094)
- M-Bossabilities™ Music embossing folder (#EL-011)
- Grand Calibur®

Additional
- Black cardstock
- Stamp sets: Faith, Hope Love...Live By It (KOM10/11), Heart and Soul (KOM 1/12)
- Assorted self-adhesive gems
- Nestabling white self-adhesive pearls: Scalloped Hearts, Hearts
- Label maker
- Black adhesive foam squares

Sources: Die templates, embossing folder and die-cutting/embossing machine from Spellbinders™ Paper Arts; cardstock from WorldWin Papers; stamp sets from Unity Stamp Co.; self-adhesive gems and Nestabling from Want2Scrap; label maker from Dymo; foam squares from SCRAPBOOK ADHESIVES BY 3L™.

Exquisite
Ornaments

Festive Ornament

DESIGN BY **CHRISTINE EMBERSON**

Using #6 Exquisite Circles die template, cut and emboss a decorative circle from patterned paper for ornament base.

Referring to Making Frames technique and using #6 and #5 Exquisite Circles die templates, cut and emboss a frame from desired color of craft foil. This will be the outside metal frame. Adhere frame to ornament base.

In the same manner, cut and emboss frame from desired color of craft foil using #4 and #3 Exquisite Circles die templates. This will be the inside metal frame. Adhere frame to ornament base.

Hand-write, or use computer and printer to generate, desired holiday sentiment onto cream cardstock. Cut a rectangle around sentiment; V-notch right end on sentiment banner. Ink edges. Adhere sentiment to ornament base.

Hand-cut two holly leaves from green felt. Adhere leaves and red beads to ornament as shown.

Thread a length of corresponding colored baker's twine through top hole of ornament; tie knot to create a hanger and trim ends. ■

Sources: Craft foil, die templates and die-cutting/embossing machine from Spellbinders™ Paper Arts; patterned paper from My Mind's Eye; baker's twine from Creative Expressions; Glossy Accents adhesive from Ranger Industries Inc.

Materials
Spellbinders™
- Precious Metals Premium Craft Foils Assortment (#F-012)
- Nestabilities® Exquisite Circles die templates (#S4-384)
- Grand Calibur®

Additional
- Cream cardstock
- Miss Caroline Lucky Tapestry patterned paper
- Green felt
- Black fine-tip marker
- Light brown ink pad
- Blue/white baker's twine
- Red beads
- Glossy Accents™ adhesive
- Computer with printer (optional)

Majestic Holiday Ornaments

DESIGN BY **KAZAN CLARK**

Adhere gold and silver craft foil sheets to black cardstock using adhesive spray. **Note:** *Adhere one foil sheet to one side of cardstock. Do not adhere foil sheets to both sides of cardstock.*

Referring to Making Frames technique and using #5 and #6 Exquisite Circles die templates, cut and emboss a frame from gold-covered cardstock. Retain center piece from die-cut frame. Repeat to cut and emboss a frame from silver-covered cardstock.

In the same manner, cut and emboss a frame from retained section of gold die-cut frame using #3 and #4 Exquisite Circles die templates. Retain center die-cut piece from die-cut frame. Repeat to cut and emboss a frame from retained section of silver die-cut frame.

In the same manner, cut and emboss a frame from retained section of gold die-cut frame using #1 and #2 Exquisite Circles die templates. Repeat to cut and emboss a frame from retained section of silver die-cut frame.

Referring to Sanding Embossed Areas technique, lightly sand all die-cut shapes to create a distressed effect. Adhere corresponding silver and gold shapes to each other so that each side is contrasted.

Punch a hole through center top and bottom of each piece except for center piece. Only punch a hole through top of center piece. Thread small lengths of wire through holes to secure shapes together.

Thread a jump ring through hole at center top of outer shape.

Repeat process using desired colors of Jewel Tones craft foils. ■

Sources: *Craft foil, die templates and die-cutting/embossing machine from Spellbinders™ Paper Arts; cardstock from American Crafts; craft wire from Artistic Wire; photo mount adhesive spray from 3M.*

Materials
Spellbinders™
- Premium Craft Foils Assortment: Precious Metals (#F-012), Jewel Tones (#F-013)
- Nestabilities® Exquisite Circles Majestic Elements die templates (#S4-384)
- Grand Calibur®

Additional
- Black cardstock
- 2 large jump rings
- 22-gauge silver craft wire
- ⅛-inch hole punch
- Sanding block
- Photo mount adhesive spray

Did You Know?
With decorative dies, it's sometimes necessary to die-cut, then rotate die 90 degrees and die-cut a second time for a complete cut.

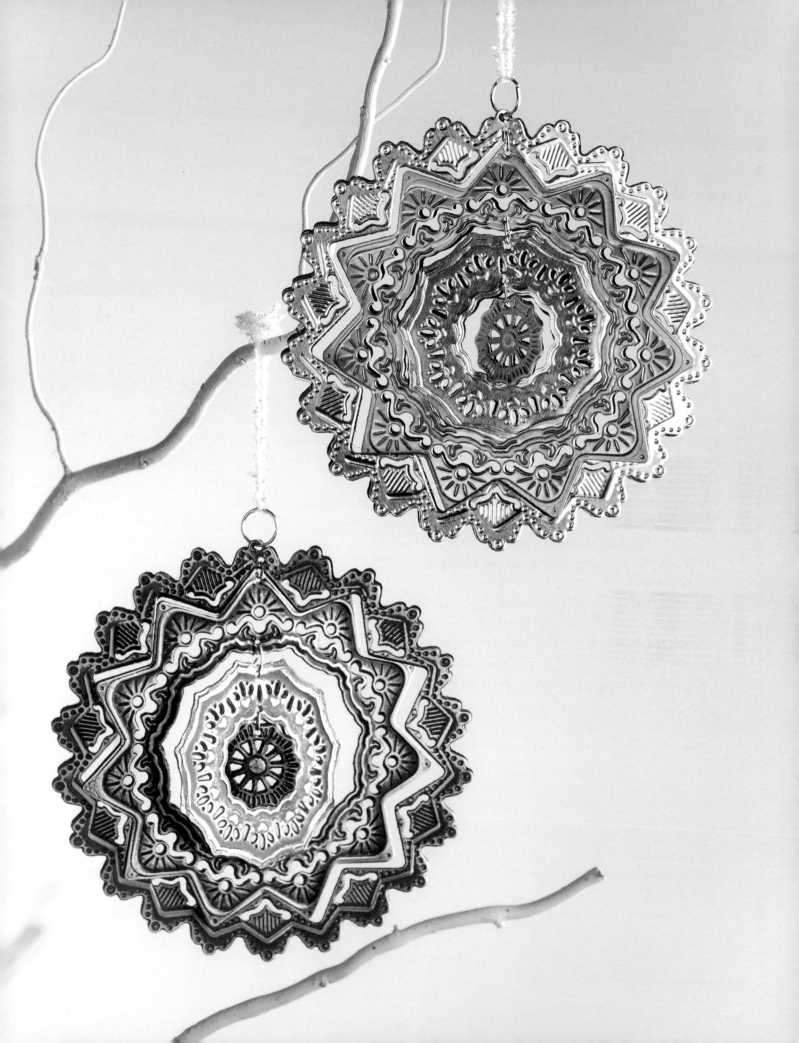

Exquisite Circles Ornament

DESIGN BY **TINA MCDONALD**

Using #6 Exquisite Circles die template, cut and emboss a decorative circle from whitewash paper, creating an ornament base.

Using #6 Standard Circles LG die template, cut two circles from cereal box cardboard. Adhere die-cut circles together using foam tape. Center and adhere to ornament base.

Using #6 and #4 Exquisite Circles die templates, cut and emboss a decorative circle from dark teal patterned paper by centering smaller die template inside larger die template. Using scissors, trim die-cut piece to separate inside circle from outside circle. Set center circle aside. Center and adhere outside circle to ornament base as shown.

In the same manner as before and using #6 and #5 Exquisite Circles die templates, cut and emboss a decorative circle from teal-striped paper. Set outer circle aside. Center and adhere inside circle to ornament as shown.

Using scoring board, score lines on points of striped outer circle. Accordion-fold along scored lines. Using hot glue, center and adhere valley folds to ornament as shown.

Using Exquisite Circles die templates #2, #3, #4 and #5, nest dies together into one circle; cut light teal paper. Rotate dies with paper in template; cut again. Repeat if necessary to get a complete cut and then emboss. Set inside circle aside.

Working with light teal outside circle, pinch small folds in between points. Curl outer points upward. Referring to photo, center and adhere to ornament using hot glue.

Adhere dark teal center circle to ornament using hot glue. Adhere light teal center circle to ornament using foam squares.

Using #2 Floral Burst die template, cut and emboss a floral burst from whitewash paper and one from reverse side of dark teal patterned paper. Trim folds from whitewash piece. With backs together, insert dark teal folds and tuck into white die-cut piece. Adhere to ornament using foam squares.

Adhere a rhinestone flower to center of ornament. Embellish ornament with pearls.

Cut a 9-inch length of ribbon. Fold one end of ribbon down 3 inches and adhere ribbon to back of ornament, creating a loop at top. Tie a bow with remaining ribbon; V-notch ends. Adhere to ribbon loop as shown. Embellish bow with rhinestone flower. ∎

Sources: *Die templates and die-cutting/embossing machine from Spellbinders™ Paper Arts; paper pads from My Mind's Eye; self-adhesive pearls from Want2Scrap; rhinestone flowers from Prima Marketing Inc.; Scor-Pal scoring board from Scor-Pal Products; foam squares from SCRAPBOOK ADHESIVES BY 3L™.*

Materials
Spellbinders™
- Nestabilities® die templates: Exquisite Circles (#S4-384), Standard Circles LG (#S4-114)
- Shapeabilities® Floral Burst die templates (#S5-113)
- Grand Calibur®

Additional
- 6 x 6-inch patterned paper pads: Lost and Found Two BREEZE, Miss Caroline FIDDLESTICKS
- Cereal box cardboard
- Small white self-adhesive pearls
- 2 aqua rhinestone flowers
- 1½-inch-wide white wire-edged satin ribbon
- Scoring board
- Hot-glue gun
- Adhesive foam squares

BUYER'S GUIDE

3M
(800) 328-6276
www.scotchbrand.com

American Crafts
(801) 226-0747
www.americancrafts.com

Art Institute Glitter
(877) 909-0805
www.artglitter.com

Artistic Wire
(610) 466-6000
www.artisticwire.com

BasicGrey
(801) 544-1116
www.basicgrey.com

Bazzill Basics Paper Inc.
(800) 560-1610
www.bazzillbasics.com

Beacon Adhesives Inc.
(914) 699-3405
www.beaconcreates.com

Bo-Bunny Press
(801) 771-4010
www.bobunny.com

Canvas Corp.
(866) 376-9961
www.canvascorp.com

Carta Bella
(855) 261-2361
www.cartabellapaper.com

Clearsnap Inc.
(800) 448-4862
www.clearsnap.com

Copic®/Imagination International Inc.
(541) 684-0013
www.copicmarker.com

Core'dinations
www.coredinations.com

Cosmo Cricket
(904)-482-0091
www.cosmocricket.com

Creative Expressions
www.creative-expressions.uk.com

Creative Imaginations
www.cigift.com

Creative Impressions Inc.
(719) 596-4860
www.creativeimpressions.com

Dick Blick Art Materials
(800) 828-4548
www.dickblick.com

Die Cuts With A View
(801) 224-6766
www.diecutswithaview.com

Dymo
(800) 640-6944
http://sites.dymo.com

Echo Park Paper Co.
(800) 701-1115
www.echoparkpaper.com

Elmer's® Products Inc.
(614) 985-2600
www.elmers.com

Etchall
(623) 933-4567
http://etchall.com/

Fiskars
(866) 348-5661
www.fiskarscrafts.com

G.C.D. Studios
(877) 272-0262
www.gcdstudios.com

Gina K. Designs
(608) 838-3258
www.ginakdesigns.com

Glue Dots
(888) 458-3368
www.gluedots.com

Graphic 45
(866) 573-4806
www.g45papers.com

Hemptique
(760) 602-3864
www.hemptique.net

Hobby Lobby Stores Inc.
www.hobbylobby.com

ICE Resin
(440) 963-0387
www.iceresin.com

Imagine Crafts/Tsukineko
(425) 883-7733
www.imaginecrafts.com

JustRite
(866) 405-6414
www.justritestampers.com

Kaisercraft
(888) 684-7147
www.kaisercraft.net

Lily Bee Design
(801) 820-6845
www.lilybeedesign.com

Lineco Inc.
(800) 322-7775
www.lineco.com

Little Yellow Bicycle
(860) 286-0244
www.mylyb.com

Maya Road
(877) 427-7764
www.mayaroad.com

May Arts
(203) 637-8366
www.mayarts.com

Melissa Frances
(877) 885-1261
www.melissafrances.com

Michaels Stores Inc.
(800) MICHAELS (642-4235)
www.michaels.com

My Mind's Eye
(800) 665-5116
www.mymindseye.com

Papertrey Ink
www.papertreyink.com

Penny Black Inc.
(800) 488-3669
www.pennyblackinc.com

Pink Paislee
(816) 298-6474
www.pinkpaislee.com

Prima Marketing Inc.
(909) 627-5532
www.primamarketinginc.com

Quick Quotes
(877) 663-7250
www.shopquickquotes.com

Quietfire Design
www.quietfiredesign.ca

Ranger Industries Inc.
(732) 389-3535
www.rangerink.com

Really Reasonable Ribbon
www.reasonableribbon.com

Royal & Langnickel
(800) 247-2211
www.royalbrush.com

The Rubber Café
(800) 991-6712
www.therubbercafe.com

Sakura of America
www.sakuraofamerica.com

Scor-Pal Products
(877) 629-9908
www.scor-pal.com

SCRAPBOOK ADHESIVES BY 3L™
www.scrapbook-adhesives.com

Shrinky Dinks®
(800) 445-7448
www.shrinkydinks.com

Spellbinders™ Paper Arts
(888) 547-0400
www.spellbinderspaperarts.com

Stampendous! Inc.
(800) 869-0474
www.stampendous.com

Stampin' Up!
(800) STAMP UP (782-6787)
www.stampinup.com

Tattered Angels
(866) 376-9961
www.mytatteredangels.com

Therm O Web Inc.
(800) 323-0799
www.thermowebonline.com

Tombow USA
www.tombowusa.com

The Twinery
http://thetwinery.com/

Unity Stamp Co.
(877) 862-2329
www.unitystampco.com

Viva Décor
www.viva-decor.us

Walnut Hollow
(800) 395-5995
www.walnuthollow.com

Want2Scrap
(260) 740-2976
www.want2scrap.com

Webster's Pages
(800) 543-6104
www.websterspages.com

Wilton Industries
(800) 794-5866
www.wilton.com

WorldWin Papers
(888) 843-6455
www.worldwinpapers.com

X-Press It
(541) 684-0013
www.copicmarker.com

Xyron Inc.
(800) 793-3523
www.xyron.com

Zutter Innovative Products
(877) 273-2818
www.zutterproducts.com

The Buyer's Guide listings are provided as a service to our readers and should not be considered an endorsement from this publication.